HOW THE BIBLE CAME TO US

LESLIE M. JOHN

"In the beginning was the Word, and the Word was with God, and the Word was God". (John 1:1)

How the Bible Came To Us

HOW THE BIBLE CAME TO US

LESLIE M. JOHN

Copyright ©2015 Leslie M. John: All rights reserved

No part of this book may be reproduced or transmitted in any form or by any means, electronic or mechanical, including photocopying, recording, or by any information storage and retrieval system, without permission in writing from the copyright owner, Leslie M. John

Unless otherwise stated the entire text in this book belongs to Leslie M. John. Credits are given to the sources on which the author depended on. Most of the images in this book are from Public Domain of which copyright is expired and are reusable. References of sources and Bibliography are cited.

The entire text of this book and graphics are deposited with Library of Congress Copyright Office, 101 Independence Avenue, SE Washington, DC 20559-6000, USA. This work is protected by Law in US; and internationally, according to The International Copyright Treatises.

ISBN-10:099078018X
ISBN-13:978-0-9907801-8-2

How the Bible Came To Us

How the Bible Came To Us

PREFACE

My mission is to proclaim the good news of our Lord Jesus Christ as revealed to me through Holy Bible and from various teachers, preachers, and commentators. This is my voluntary service to God in the name of His only begotten Son Lord Jesus Christ.

I share the truth of knowledge of God with others with good intention of bringing them to the knowledge of the living God, the God of Abraham, the God of Isaac, the God of Jacob, and the Father of our Lord Jesus Christ. My mission is to proclaim the Gospel of Lord Jesus Christ and not converting forcibly anyone to Christianity.

There are fundamental Christian doctrines that I believe in and I will not compromise on those doctrines. They are:

God is Triune: The Father, The Son and The Holy Spirit. They are not three Gods, but One God in three persons, co-equal-co-existent and functionally different.

There is no salvation except by Grace through Faith in Lord Jesus Christ. I believe in:

"That if thou shalt confess with thy mouth the Lord Jesus, and shalt believe in thine heart that God hath raised him from the dead, thou shalt be saved" (Romans 10:9)

One may accept or reject any or part of my writings/teachings. No offense is meant to any individual or any religion or any organization. Please visit http://www.lesliejohn.net/

How the Bible Came To Us

I pray for the peace of Jerusalem and desire that all Jews may accept Lord Jesus as their personal Savior and Messiah.

"Pray for the peace of Jerusalem: they shall prosper that love thee" (Psalms 122:6)

I firmly believe in the saying of Jesus, who said:

"No man can come to me, except the Father which hath sent me draw him: and I will raise him up at the last day" John 6:44.

My efforts to teach or preach are of no use unless Lord Jesus Christ Himself intervenes and the Father draws a person unto Him.

All Scriptures in electronic format are from King James Version (KJV) from Open domain, and

English Standard Version (ESV)

The Holy Bible, English Standard Version Copyright © 2001 by Crossway Bibles, a division of Good News Publishers.

Disclaimer:

No offence is meant to any individual, or religion, or any organization practicing any other beliefs than that of the author.

Description:

The Holy Bible, which is the inspired, inerrant, and infallible Word of God, was under attack for many centuries now. The very first attack by Satan on the Word of God was when he came in the form of serpent and asked Eve a cunning question

How the Bible Came To Us

saying "Yea, hath God said, Ye shall not eat of every tree of the garden?"

Satan has been raising questions in the minds of innocent people from that day onward until this day and will continue to ask such questions till the end of the world.

This book deals with how God's inspired Word came to us in written form.

"God, who at sundry times and in divers manners spake in time past unto the fathers by the prophets, Hath in these last days spoken unto us by his Son, whom he hath appointed heir of all things, by whom also he made the worlds; Who being the brightness of his glory, and the express image of his person, and upholding all things by the word of his power, when he had by himself purged our sins, sat down on the right hand of the Majesty on high" (Hebrews 1:1-3)

If someone points to the fact that there are no originals now, and what we have are copies of copies, then Hebrews 1:1-3 should tell us that if God's Word which He spoke to the prophets was written down, and that which was transmitted from Him to the subsequent writers chosen by Him was true and believable, then the scribes who collected fragments, vellum or parchments, or papyri and worked them diligently for many years putting together should be believed.

Even though there were errors in compiling the text from the fragments into Codices, and then to the Printable Bible that we have today, the central theme that "God is love" and He sent His only Son into this world that whosoever believes in Him shall not perish but have everlasting life, never changed.

How the Bible Came To Us

How the Bible Came To Us

Contents

HOW THE BIBLE CAME TO US 1

PREFACE 5

SECTION I HOW THE BIBLE CAME TO US 15

INTRODUCTION..17

CHAPTER 1 THE ORIGIN 20

CHAPTER 2 DEVELOPMENT OF SCRIPT 24

    THE TYPES OF TEXTS 25

    THE ALEXANDRIAN TEXT 27

    THE BYZANTIAN TEXT...27

    THE WESTERN TEXT 27

    THE CASEREAN TEXT 27

CHAPTER 3 LANGUAGE AND THE TEXT 29

    DEFINITIONS 29

    PAPYRUS 29

    CODEX 29

    PARCHMENT OR VELLUM 29

    LANGUAGE 30

    TEXT 30

    MANUSCRIPT 30

. CHAPTER 4 CAIN BUILT A CITY 31

CHAPTER 5 EGYPTIAN PYRAMIDS AND ISRAELITES............34

CHAPTER 6 MOSES AND HIS SKILLS.....................................37

CHAPTER 7 TORAH AND ITS AUTHOR 41

How the Bible Came To Us

CHAPTER 8 MASORETES AND MASORETIC TEXT 46
    EARLY SCRIPT AND TANAKH 46

CHAPTER 9 SEPTUAGINT 50
    BACKGROUND 50
    THE SEVENTY 51

CHAPTER 10 SCRIPTURES AND SCROLLS 54

CHAPTER 11 NEW TESTAMENT AND THE LANGUAGE 57

A NEW TESTAMENT FRAGMENT 60
    NEW TESTAMENT PAPYRI 60

CHAPTER 12 GOD SPOKE THROUGH PROPHETS 64

CHAPTER 13 TEXTUAL CRITICISM 68

TEXTUS RECEPTUS 72

ERASMUS TEXT: LAST PAGE REV22 8 21.jpg 72

CHAPTER 14 THE LIFE OF JESUS 73

CHAPTER 15 THE CODICES 75
    AN IMPORTANT YEAR 76

CHAPTER 16 VULGATE BIBLE 79

CHAPTER 17 CODEX SINAITICUS 84

CHAPTER 18 CODEX VATICANUS 88

PAGE FROM ALEPPO CODEX DEUTERONOMY 92

CHAPTER 19 APOCRYPHA BOOKS 93

CHAPTER 20 INERRANCY AND INFALLIBILTY 96
    INERRANCY 96
    HEBREW LANGUAGE 97

How the Bible Came To Us

- INFALLIBILITY 98
- CHAPTER 21 THE TRANSMISSION 100
  - IMPERFECT TRANSMISSION 101
- CHAPTER 22 DEAD SEA SCROLLS 102
- CHAPTER 23 THE GIST OF APOCRYPHA BOOKS..............105
  - APOCRYPHA BOOKS 105
  - 1 ESDRAS 107
  - 2 ESDRAS 108
  - TOBIT 108
  - JUDITH 109
  - ADDITIONS TO ESTHER 110
  - WISDOM OF SOLOMON..111
  - ECCLESIASTICUS 111
  - BARUCH 112
  - LETTER OF JEREMIAH 115
  - PRAYER OF AZARIAH 116
  - SUSANNA 117
  - BEL AND THE DRAGON 118
  - THE PRAYER OF MANASSEH...................................120
  - FIRST MACCABEES 123
  - SECOND MACCABEES...123
  - THIRD AND FOURTH MACCABEES...........................124
- CHAPTER 24 THE BANNED BOOKS 125
  - UNCOMPROMSING STORIES...................................126

How the Bible Came To Us

APOCRYPHAL BOOKS	126
THE LIFE OF ADAM AND EVE	128
THE BOOK OF JUBILEES	129
THE BOOK OF ENOCH	131
THE GOSPEL OF THOMAS	131
THE PROTOVANGELION OF JAMES	132
THE GOSPEL OF MARY MAGDALENE	133
THE GOSPEL OF NICODEMUS	134
THE APOCALYPSE OF PETER	137
CHAPTER 25 NEW TESTAMENT CANON	139
THE NEW TESTAMENT	139
CHAPTER 26 APOSTLE PAUL'S MISSIONARY WORK	143
POINTS IN CONCISE	143
FIRST MISSIONARY JOURNEY	143
SECOND MISSIONARY JOURNEY	144
THIRD MISSIONARY JOURNEY	145
JOURNEY TO ROME	146
PAUL'S FIRST ROMAN IMPRISONMENT	147
PAUL'S SECOND ROMAN IMPRISONMENT	147
CHAPTER 27 CANONIZATION OF THE BIBLE	148
CHAPTER 28 THE DEVELOPMENT	151
LEADING TO NEW TESTAMENT CANON	151
CLEMENT OF ROME	153
POLYCARP	154

How the Bible Came To Us

    IRENAEUS 157

    TERTULLIAN 161

    ATHANASIUS 163

CHAPTER 29 CRITERIA FOR CANONIZATION 166

    INTENT OF SCRIPTURE 166

    BARJESUS 167

    MARCION 168

    TEST THE SPIRITS 169

    SCRIPTURE 170

CHAPTER 30 ROLE OF CONSTANTINE 174

    THE COUNCIL OF NICAEA 175

CHAPTER 31 THREE THOUSAND YEARS IN NUTSHELL 184

    FIRST WRITTEN WORD 184

    THE SEPTUAGINT 184

    THE NEW TESTAMENT 184

    COUNCIL OF NICAEA 185

    JOHN WYCLIFFE BIBLE 185

    MARTIN LUTHER'S BIBLE 185

    PRINTING PRESS 186

    ERASMUS BIBLE 186

    WILLIAM TYNDALE BIBLE 186

    THE GREAT BIBLE 187

    MYLES COVERDALE BIBLE 187

    GENEVA BIBLE 187

How the Bible Came To Us

1611 AUTHORIZED VERSION (KING JAMES BIBLE)	188
SECTION II SALVATION MESSAGES	190
CHAPTER 32 SAVED BY GRACE	191
CHAPTER 33 GOD LIVES IN OUR HEARTS	194
CHAPTER 34 PETER AND JOHN TESTIFY	197
CHAPTER 35 UNLESS YOU BELIEVE	201
BIBLIOGRAPHY	205

SECTION I
HOW THE BIBLE CAME TO US

How the Bible Came To Us

How the Bible Came To Us

INTRODUCTION

The Holy Bible, which is the inspired, inerrant, and infallible Word of God, was under attack for many centuries now. The very first attack by Satan on the Word of God was when he came in the form of serpent and asked Eve a cunning question saying "Yea, hath God said, Ye shall not eat of every tree of the garden?"

Satan has been raising questions in the minds of innocent people from that day onward until this day and will continue to ask such questions till the end of the world.

In spite of God blessing Adam and Eve and said to them to be "fruitful, and multiply, and replenish the earth, and subdue it: and have dominion over the fish of the sea, and over the fowl of the air, and over every living thing that moveth upon the earth" and lead a happy life in the garden that he planted eastward in Eden eating of every tree of the garden freely except of the tree of knowledge of good and evil, man fell Adam and Eve fell victim to the temptation of Satan.

God warned them that "in the day that thou eatest thereof thou shalt surely die" but Eve and Adam ate of the forbidden tree and found that they were naked. They lost spiritual fellowship with God and were chased out of the Garden of Eden.

Man has been, since then, doubting as to how the Bible came to be and is what is written in the word of God true or not. Ever since the written Word of God came into the hands of Christians there has been constant attack saying that the Bible is written by few men, it has errors and revised several times etc.

How the Bible Came To Us

Questions keep arising without ceasing as to how some minor errors such as spelling mistakes or words that lead to difference in interpretations have crept into the Bible.

The Word of God is God-breathed, infallible and inerrant, and yet while translating the original texts into various languages human capability played a great role.

It is to be borne in mind that even though there was disputes in some areas of the Bible, the central doctrine God is love and salvation is by grace through faith in Lord Jesus Christ, who paid the price for our salvation by offering Himself as sacrifice and dying on the cross and coming out of the grave alive and ascending into heaven is never changed.

It is imperative that every Christian should have knowledge as to how the Bible came to us. A large number of Christians do not know why they believe what they believe, either because they have pre-notion that whatever was taught to them is right or they are not interested to find out the truth.

Careful study of the history of the Bible and comparison of the truths of the Bible with others' beliefs in God would help understand how great is the Bible, and how true is the Yahweh, the only God, by whose only Son's death on the cross and resurrection we have hope that our inner soul will not die but be with Him forever and ever in glorified bodies.

Dust that we are we will return to dust but our souls are not lost forever either in the "lake of fire" or come back to this earth once again incarnating probably as cat, rat or crow.

I wonder of the hopelessness the man who replied to me once said that he will see what he would be after his death. He will

How the Bible Came To Us

surely see himself in eternal fire just as the rich man saw himself in in hell while his servant Lazarus was in Abraham's bosom. One may have pleasure, wealth, and power in this life, but the truth is that by not asking forgiveness of sins from Lord Jesus one will not receive salvation.

The Bible asks a simple question...

"For what is a man profited, if he shall gain the whole world, and lose his own soul? or what shall a man give in exchange for his soul?" (Matthew 16:26)

The rich on this earth would be paupers in heaven while the poor on this earth, who have acknowledged by mouth that Jesus as Lord and believed in heart that God raised Him from the dead will be rich in heaven. Bible says gather treasure in heaven where moth does not corrupt our possessions.

How the Bible Came To Us

CHAPTER 1
THE ORIGIN

"In the beginning was the Word, and the Word was with God, and the Word was God". (John 1:1)

With the passage of time the Word of God is revealed through various men of God; however, it was in the beginning, and it was with God, and the Word was God. His Word rises for the oppression of the poor, for the relief of the needy, and to set them in safety. They are as pure as silver tried in a furnace of earth seven times.

Bible is a collection of sixty six Books; 39 of the Old Testament and 27 or the New Testament. Forty men wrote the books of the Bible, spanning a period of about 1600 years, from time period of Moses (1500 BC) to the time period of John (AD 97), who wrote the Book of Revelation.

Forty men who wrote the books were Kings, Poets, Shepherds and Philosophers. Even though one writer did not know the other, every scribe was guided and supervised by the Holy Spirit, and that is the reason why the Bible has become so great book in the world. Not a single book lasted so long as the Bible did, and yet it is so pure and fresh. Repeated listening of the messages from the Bible does not wear us out, but it refreshes our souls and minds.

"For the prophecy came not in old time by the will of man: but holy men of God spake as they were moved by the Holy Ghost" (2 Peter 1:21)

How the Bible Came To Us

When Nebuchadnezzar was full of fury he ordered the furnace to be heated seven times more than it usually is heated. Shadrach, Meshach and Abednego, who were thrown into that fiery furnace, came out of it without being harmed.

Similarly, even though the word of God is tested to the best of fury of its opponents, it comes out purified greatly to increase in abundance (cf. Daniel 3:19; Psalms 12:6; Psalms 12:5)

Since the time the written Word of God (The Bible) came into our hands, many challenged it disapproving its veracity and reliability, but such oppositions came to be rested in peace. It is misunderstanding that the word of God changed or altered several times, nay, the Word of God never changed or altered, but with the passage of time it is presented in more understandable formats. Some felt King James Version is hard to understand while many felt it was the more reliable version.

The scriptures were written first on papyrus, and then as the development took place it was written on the scrolls of parchments that were made of animal skins. Scripting developed from pictorial representations to hieroglyph, and then to calligraphy with pen and in styles in cursive formats to that of print media now available in various versions.

The timeline of events from Abraham to the time of Emperor Constantine forms the core period of unearthing vital documents that relate to the compilation of various books of the Bible into one book. Bible and history records the transcending periods of judges, kings, poets and philosophers.

The timeline from Abraham to Emperor Constantine is important to be taken note of; because it was during the period of Emperor Constantine that a major decision was taken as to

How the Bible Came To Us

how much of unprofitable writings, or personal opinions, and heretical writings were to be rejected from being conflated into one great book that serves the purpose of holy living.

- Abraham (in 17th Century B.C)
- Moses
- The children of Israel
- King Saul
- King David
- King Solomon
- Division of Solomon's kingdom into two - Southern Kingdom of Judah under Rehoboam and Northern Kingdom of Israel under Jeroboam
- 20 Kings of Judah from Rehoboam
- 19 Kings of Israel from Jeroboam
- King Nebuchadnezzar's rule
- Babylonian captivity of Southern Kingdom
- Assyrian captivity of Northern Kingdom
- Scattering of the House of Israel
- Persian and Hellenistic periods
- Return of Jews and rebuilding of the Temple
- Conquest of Alexander the great
- Maccabean revolt
- Roman Rule
- Byzantine Rule under Constantine
- Persian Invasion
- Arab Rule
- Crusader domination
- Mamluk Rule
- Ottaman Rule
- British Rule
- State of Israel came into existence in 1948

How the Bible Came To Us

It was during Emperor Constantine's time that a council was called at a place called Nicene. 400 years of silence after Prophets and Kings the Lord was born. John the Baptist was the last Prophet who was before Jesus and was killed by Herod during the time period of Lord Jesus

How the Bible Came To Us

CHAPTER 2
DEVELOPMENT OF SCRIPT

In the Old Testament period the script was first written on Papyrus made of pith of the material that was used to make the basket to keep Moses safe at the banks of Nile river when the King of Egypt ordered killing of all Hebrew babies as their mothers gave birth to them. The script gradually developed from hieroglyph to modern text on paper to digital formats. During the process of development of civilization and the script from primitive format to digital formats, human element played a great role. It made difference even when a comma was placed at a wrong place in a sentence.

The Scriptures were inspired by God, but He did not supervise the translations, and consequently minor errors such as placing of commas in a wrong place in a sentence by humans, rendered different interpretation. Nevertheless, the gist and the main theme remained unchanged. For example, in Matthew 3:3 we find the scripture as

"... The voice of one crying in the wilderness, Prepare ye the way of the Lord, make his paths straight" (Matthew 3:3)

The Septuagint had it as "The voice of one crying, In the wilderness prepare the way for the Lord". Thus the difference in interpretations could be observed. In the latter case the one who was crying in the wilderness could be, could not be in the wilderness, but in the former necessarily one who was crying in the wilderness was in the wilderness. The prophecy in KJV Isaiah 40:3 reads "The voice of him that crieth in the wilderness,

How the Bible Came To Us

Prepare ye the way of the LORD, make straight in the desert a highway for our God" (Isaiah 40:3)

Even if one takes the interpretation of the verbatim Septuagint, the essence of the declaration that John the Baptist was the forerunner of Lord Jesus does not change. Yet there are few who consider such minor deviations as enough proof to brand Bible as erratic. Even though the central message does not deviate from the truth yet they oppose Christianity.

THE TYPES OF TEXTS

The New Testament is written in Greek Language. From the text of the manuscripts found it was seen that the local people and their language had great impact on the presentation of the language. After ascension of Lord Jesus Christ the Gospel of Jesus Christ was communicated very fast, first to people in Jerusalem, and then to Judea and Samaria and then to the uttermost parts of the earth. Even as Christianity spread across the globe many thousands accepted Lord Jesus Christ as their savior in the early centuries.

The verbal communication was in different language followed by the New Testament scripture that was written in Greek from the manuscripts of the apostles and other writers. Later on the New Testament from Greek was translated into several languages in the world making it the only book to have been translated into such great record number of languages.

The best of the dedicated Godly Scholars available during those days first wrote the New Testament based on their dependence on the different types of texts available to them from the manuscripts to match in the best possible way with the original thoughts of the writers, who left behind them the life of Lord

How the Bible Came To Us

Jesus Christ, His works, His death, His burial, His Resurrection and His ascension. The New Testament as we know today contains not only four Gospels but also epistles from apostles and Revelation (apocalypse).

While the scholars perused the manuscripts available to them they found that there were four types of texts used in the manuscripts. The four types of texts found in the New Testament manuscripts were broadly classified into four groups identified as families. The deviations identified in the texts of different families were peculiar to their ancestor family.

Therefore, textual reconstruction had to take note of the departure from the original text by different families, and thus the misleading texts from the poor families was eliminated or modifications rendered to match as close to the thoughts of the apostles[1] as possible. There was no Bible in print format until the first print Bible was made available in 1455 AD by Johannes Gutenberg[2], a German, who was blacksmith and the first man to introduce printing in Europe.

In all these exercises God was with them to put His word as He wanted while canonizing the Bible; nevertheless, human element forced into the texts, some errors of placement of punctuations or spelling errors .

The four types of texts that were found in the New Testament manuscripts were...

---

[1] "The infallible rule of interpretation of Scripture is the Scripture itself: and therefore, when there is a question about the true and full sense of any Scripture (which is not manifold, but one), it must be searched and known by other places that speak more clearly" THE WESTMINSTER CONFESSION OF FAITH CHAPTER 1 PARA 9
[2] Wikipedia - Johannes Gutenberg

How the Bible Came To Us

1. THE ALEXANDRIAN TEXT
2. THE BYZANTIAN TEXT
3. THE WESTERN TEXT and
4. THE CAESAREAN TEXT

THE ALEXANDRIAN TEXT – Alexandria was in Egypt and the region was dominated by the culture of the people that belonged to the time period of Alexander the great, who was king of Macedonia conquering Greece and reestablishing the Corinthians League, and conquering Persian Empire. This type of text was used in the earliest form of Greek New Testament and was written in upper case letters known as Uncials. However, the modern text used remix of Greek text called "Eclectic Greek". Alexandrian Text had little scope to paraphrase and some manuscripts had Byzantine corrections[3]

THE BYZANTIAN TEXT – It is so called because it was adopted by Constantinople in the Byzantine region for general use and it became almost universal language in eighth century. Erasmus and King James Version publishers used this type text for the first Greek printed version of the Bible.

THE WESTERN TEXT – was used in western Churches and could be traced to second century.

THE CASEREAN TEXT – was used in Caesarea and possibly it was a remix of Alexandrian text and Western text, and therefore, lost its importance[4].

---

[3] Papyrus 66, Codex Sinaiticus, Codex Ephraemi, Codex Regius, and Codex Sangallensis - Wikipedia
[4] Bruce M. Metzger, *The Text of the New Testament*, p. 215)
Credits to: R. C. Briggs, *Interpreting the New Testament Today: An Introduction to Methods and Issues in the Study of the New Testament*, (Nashville: Abingdon, 1982), pp. 45-47).

How the Bible Came To Us

CHAPTER 3
LANGUAGE AND THE TEXT

DEFINITIONS [5]

PAPYRUS

1. a tall, aquatic plant, *Cyperus papyrus,* of the sedge family, native to the Nile valley: the Egyptian subspecies, *C. papyrus hadidii,* thought to be common in ancient times, now occurs only in several sites.

2. a material on which to write, prepared from thin strips of the pith of this plant laid together, soaked, pressed, and dried, used by the ancient Egyptians, Greeks, and Romans.

3. An ancient document, manuscript, or scroll written on this material.

CODEX

1. A quire of manuscript pages held together by stitching: the earliest form of book, replacing the scrolls and wax tablets of earlier times.

2. a manuscript volume, usually of an ancient classic or the Scriptures

PARCHMENT OR VELLUM

1. The skin of sheep, goats, etc., prepared for use as a material on which to write.

---

[5] "dictionary." *Online Etymology Dictionary.* Douglas Harper, Historian. 22 May. 2015.

How the Bible Came To Us

2. A manuscript or document on such material.

LANGUAGE

"A body of words and the systems for their use common to a people who are of the same community or nation, the same geographical area, or the same cultural tradition"

TEXT

It is the main body of matter in a manuscript, book, newspaper, etc., as distinguished from notes, appendixes, headings, illustrations, etc.

MANUSCRIPT

The original text of an author's work, handwritten or now usually typed, that is submitted to a publisher

How the Bible Came To Us

. CHAPTER 4
CAIN BUILT A CITY

"And Cain knew his wife; and she conceived, and bare Enoch: and he builded a city, and called the name of the city, after the name of his son, Enoch" (Genesis 4:17)

It is marvelous to think that God communed verbally with Adam and Eve and likewise Adam communicated with Eve, and Serpent communicated with Adam and Eve verbally. However, it is not too much to think Adam could have drawn a picture of fruit on the ground to say something to Eve and that picture could have given more meaningful interpretation of what he wanted to say. It is not documented in the Bible, of course, but it is not beyond one's conjecture.

Later on the Scriptures record that Cain built a city. It was one of the best evidences that there was communication either by symbols or by script. Cain built a city and called it "Enoch" after the name of his son. There can be no city built without proper planning, without the design, and structure that would involve mathematical numbers.

Much later, during the period when Israelites were led by Moses the servant of God, they were given Ten Commandments. Bible says God wrote The Ten Commandments with His finger; the finger being metaphorical expression, of course, because God is a Spirit and no man has seen Him, and He does not have physical structure. Nevertheless, He wrote and there was the script and the script was engraved on the stone, never to get erased. Moses, in his anger, broke the two stone tablets containing the Ten

How the Bible Came To Us

Commandments because he saw the children of Israel were worshipping an idol. However, God wrote the Ten Commandments second time and gave to Moses to read and speak to the children of Israel. Obviously, Moses and the children of Israel were able to read what was written by God on the stone tablets.

"And he gave unto Moses, when he had made an end of communing with him upon mount Sinai, two tables of testimony, tables of stone, written with the finger of God" (Exodus 31:18)

It is not by coincidence that the sixty six books in the Bible have been put together. They are there in the Bible by divine ordination. Although most of the books in the Bible except the first five books in the Old Testament and epistles in the New Testament, are written by different authors unknown to one another, yet the details of the Bible matched wonderfully. The first five books were written by Moses much later after the children of Israel left Egypt.

The archaeological evidences, the historical evidences of men, kings, fishermen, poets and many others who wrote the books in the Bible goes to show that the scriptures are inspired. God, who out breathed His Word is the author of the Holy Bible and human beings were used as instruments in His hands to convey His mind. Thus the scriptures are inspired and they were written down when God out breathed His word through men. . Lord Jesus Christ called the writings as "Scriptures" and they are given for us to understand God, His attributes and His nature.

There was no script when Heavens and Earth were created by God and similarly there was no script when Adam and Eve were created by God. The question obviously is who wrote that

How the Bible Came To Us

serpent was subtle among all the beasts of the earth and it deceived Eve. Adam participated in the transgression by Eve of the command of God, thus rendering themselves as sinners before God. Sin was inherited by all their descendants because they represented the whole humanity.

It was by the hand of Moses that the first five books, called Pentateuch, of the Bible were written. Moses was born to Hebrew parents and because Pharaoh was seeking to kill all Hebrews Moses was by divine plan was taken into Pharaoh's house, where he grew under his mother, who was unknowingly appointed by Pharaoh to bring up Moses, who learnt all the skills and gained intelligence in Pharaoh's house.

CHAPTER 5
EGYPTIAN PYRAMIDS AND ISRAELITES

Egyptian Pyramids[6] were one of the seven wonders in the world, built between 2600 BC and 2500 BC. The twelfth dynasty of Pharaoh used the slave force of Israelites to construct the pyramids[7].

During the period of Joseph the children of Israel prospered and later as the time passed by a new king arose who did not know who Joseph was. The king envied the children of Israel as they grew stronger and mightier and therefore, set up taskmasters to afflict them.

The children of Israel built cities namely Pithom and Raamses for Pharaoh. God was with the children of Israel, and therefore, the more the Egyptians afflicted them the more they multiplied and grew. Egyptians made the children of Israel serve them with rigor (cf. Exodus 1:8-13).

Not only the Bible gives the accuracies of these details but the historian Flavius Joseph also records the details in Para 1 of Chapter 9 of Book II of Josephus - Antiquities of the Jews.

---

[6] 1 Maccabees 13:28; compare Josephus Ant, XIII vi, 6

[7] Flavius Josephus. Antiquities, II:9.1 "And having, in length of time, forgotten the benefits they had received from Joseph, particularly the crown being now come into another family, they became very abusive to the Israelites, and contrived many ways of afflicting them; for they enjoined them to cut a great number of channels for the river, and to build walls for their cities and ramparts, that they might restrain the river, and hinder its waters from stagnating, upon its running over its own banks: they set them also to build pyramids..."

How the Bible Came To Us

Exodus Chapter 1 records how Pharaoh planned to kill male children of Israelites but the two midwives, "Shiphrah" and "Puah" appointed by the king to kill male children feared God, and had sympathy towards male children and spared them. When they were questioned of their action they replied that the Hebrew women were livelier than the Hebrew women and they gave birth to children before they went into kill them.

Exodus Chapter 2 records the birth and upbringing of Moses. A man from the tribe of "Levi" married a woman from the same tribe and they had a son, who was Moses. When the woman saw that the child was exceedingly good, she hid him three months.

"And the woman conceived, and bare a son: and when she saw him that he was a goodly child, she hid him three months" (Exodus 2:2)

"In which time Moses was born, and was exceeding fair, and nourished up in his father's house three months" Acts 7:20

When the mother of Moses could no longer hide the baby Moses she made basket with bulrushes and daubed it with bitumen and pitch. She placed the child gently in the basket and the basket among the reeds by the river bank. Pharaoh's daughter comes there for a bath and finds the baby and takes it to the palace, where baby Moses grows to adulthood. Incidentally the mother of Moses was hired to rear the child and thus Moses was looked after by God.

Surprisingly this raw material became the source for papyrus on which the Egyptians did scripting. The details of Papyrus and hieroglyphics are not described here because it involves seeking permission from various sources.

How the Bible Came To Us

Dictionary defines "Papyrus" as a tall aquatic plant native of Nile Valley an Egyptian subspecies, a material on which to write, prepared from thin strips of the pith of this plant laid together, soaked, pressed, and dried, used by the ancient Egyptians, Greeks, and Romans. It is an ancient document, manuscript, or scroll written on this material.

Dictionary defines "hieroglyphics" as "designating or pertaining to a pictographic script, particularly that of the ancient Egyptians, in which many of the symbols are conventionalized, recognizable pictures of the things represented".

How the Bible Came To Us

CHAPTER 6
MOSES AND HIS SKILLS

And when he was cast out, Pharaoh's daughter took him up, and nourished him for her own son. And Moses was learned in all the wisdom of the Egyptians, and was mighty in words and in deeds. (Acts 7:21-22)

Stephen recounting before high priest spoke of Moses, who spent his childhood and youth in the house of Pharaoh of Egypt, where the children of Israel were slaves and were persecuted. Pharaoh's daughter loved Moses, who was carefully nursed by his mother Jochebed. Moses, while growing in the house of the most powerful man in the land, "learned in all the wisdom of the Egyptians, and was mighty in words and in deeds".

"Then said his sister to Pharaoh's daughter, Shall I go and call to thee a nurse of the Hebrew women, that she may nurse the child for thee? And Pharaoh's daughter said to her, Go. And the maid went and called the child's mother. And Pharaoh's daughter said unto her, Take this child away, and nurse it for me, and I will give thee thy wages. And the woman took the child, and nursed it. And the child grew, and she brought him unto Pharaoh's daughter, and he became her son. And she called his name Moses: and she said, Because I drew him out of the water" (Exodus 2:7-10)

Bible does not give the dates of Moses's birth and death; however, it does give some evidence as to when he lived and the year when the Exodus took place. Moses was eighty years old when the children of Israel left Egypt from their bondage of slavery.

How the Bible Came To Us

"Now Moses was eighty years old, and Aaron eighty-three years old, when they spoke to Pharaoh" (Exodus 7:7 ESV)

"In the four hundred and eightieth year after the people of Israel came out of the land of Egypt, in the fourth year of Solomon's reign over Israel, in the month of Ziv, which is the second month, he began to build the house of the LORD" (1 Kings 6:1 ESV)

Egyptians were excellent in astrology, in interpretation of dreams, in medicine, in mathematics, and in religion; however King Solomon's wisdom surpassed their wisdom (cf. 1 Kings 4:30).

"Philip found Nathanael and said to him, 'We have found him of whom Moses in the Law and also the prophets wrote, Jesus of Nazareth, the son of Joseph.'" (John 1:45 ESV)

Lord Jesus Christ spoke of Moses and said he wrote about the Lord

"For had ye believed Moses, ye would have believed me: for he wrote of me" (John 5:46)

In all these, it shows that Moses had good knowledge in Egyptian hieroglyphs and during those days Papyrus was used to draw pictures on and write letters.

Way back in Genesis 3.15 there is a prophecy about Lord Jesus Christ that he would come into this world born of a woman and He will crush the head of the seed of the woman. Moses wrote about Lord Jesus
Christ that God will raise Him up as a prophet in the midst of the children of Israel and that they would hearken unto Him. Recalling the Scriptures Samaritan woman said to Lord Jesus

How the Bible Came To Us

Christ that she perceived him as the one who is spoken of as a prophet.

"And I will put enmity between thee and the woman, and between thy seed and her seed; it shall bruise thy head, and thou shalt bruise his heel" (Genesis 3:15)

"The LORD thy God will raise up unto thee a Prophet from the midst of thee, of thy brethren, like unto me; unto him ye shall hearken" (Deuteronomy 18:15)

"Art thou greater than our father Jacob, which gave us the well, and drank thereof himself, and his children, and his cattle?" (John 4:12)

"The woman saith unto him, Sir, I perceive that thou art a prophet" (John 4:19)

"The woman said to him, 'I know that Messiah is coming (he who is called Christ). When he comes, he will tell us all things.'" (John 4:25 ESV)

Scholars have researched and found the Moses wrote the first five books of the Bible that are called as "Torah" or "Pentateuch".

Noah had to obey God's command and build an ark to get saved. There are types and shadows in the Old Testament period and they were fulfilled in the substances (Anti-types and realities) in the New Testament period.

"For as by one man's disobedience many were made sinners, so by the obedience of one shall many be made righteous" (Romans 5:19)

How the Bible Came To Us

By One man's transgression the sin entered the world, and by one man's death on the cross that sin had to be paid for. He was not mere man, who died but He was the "Everlasting Father" as described in Isaiah 9:6.

How the Bible Came To Us

CHAPTER 7
TORAH AND ITS AUTHOR

God is the author of the Bible and that is to mean He is the author of the first five books in the Bible as well; however, it is Moses who put them in script for us to read. God used Moses to convey His heart, His mind and His thoughts and Moses wrote down that which God commanded Him to write. The greatest evidence that Moses wrote Torah (Pentateuch – the first five books; Genesis, Exodus, Leviticus, Numbers, and Deuteronomy) is in the words of none other than Lord Jesus Christ, who said Moses wrote about Him.

The writings in the Torah[8] are in two forms, the first being as God instructing Moses to write, and the second being Moses speaks as he wrote the books. Some understand in ignorance, or deliberately misinterpret based on this two way presentation that Moses did not write Torah. Such objections are trivial and purely biased. They are to be thwarted away because there are ample evidences in the Bible and in the writings of Jewish historians that Moses wrote the Torah.

If the reader does not believe it so, the onus of proving otherwise is on him. It is for him to show as to why he does not believe that Moses wrote Pentateuch, and who that other person is who wrote Torah. Jesus said...

"For had ye believed Moses, ye would have believed me: for he wrote of me" (John 5:46)Moses claimed that he was commanded by the LORD to write the LORD's words and hid did as he was commanded to do. If one claims as the author of a

---

[8] *"Torah"*, Wikipedia, n.d. Web [17 Apr, 2015]

book then he should be believed unless his claim could be proved wrong. One also should be in a position to prove the Scriptures are wrong.

"And the LORD said unto Moses, Write thou these words: for after the tenor of these words I have made a covenant with thee and with Israel" (Exodus 34:27)

The defeat of Amalekites was a significant historical evidence to take into cognizance as to how Moses's hand was kept raised towards God by Aaron and Hur standing on his either side seeking in prayer the victory for the children of Israel over mighty Amalekites. God heard their prayer and helped Israel to defeat Amalekites.

"And Moses built an altar and called the name of it, The LORD Is My Banner, saying, "A hand upon the throne of the LORD! The LORD will have war with Amalek from generation to generation." (Exodus 17:15-16 ESV)

Flavius Josephus Antiquities of the Jews Book 3 Chapter 2 describes in detail as to how Moses's intervention led to the victory of the children of Israel over Amalekites. The LORD instructed Moses to write the details of that great victory for a memorial in a book.

And the LORD said unto Moses, Write this for a memorial in a book, and rehearse it in the ears of Joshua: for I will utterly put out the remembrance of Amalek from under heaven. (Exodus 17:14)

There are several references quoting Moses as the writer of the first five books of the Bible.

How the Bible Came To Us

"These are the journeys of the children of Israel, which went forth out of the land of Egypt with their armies under the hand of Moses and Aaron. And Moses wrote their goings out according to their journeys by the commandment of the LORD: and these are their journeys according to their goings out" (Numbers 33:1-2)

"And Moses wrote this law, and delivered it unto the priests the sons of Levi, which bare the ark of the covenant of the LORD, and unto all the elders of Israel" (Deuteronomy 31:9)

"Only be thou strong and very courageous, that thou mayest observe to do according to all the law, which Moses my servant commanded thee: turn not from it to the right hand or to the left, that thou mayest prosper whithersoever thou goest. This book of the law shall not depart out of thy mouth; but thou shalt meditate therein day and night, that thou mayest observe to do according to all that is written therein: for then thou shalt make thy way prosperous, and then thou shalt have good success" (Joshua 1:7-8)

"And keep the charge of the LORD thy God, to walk in his ways, to keep his statutes, and his commandments, and his judgments, and his testimonies, as it is written in the law of Moses, that thou mayest prosper in all that thou doest, and whithersoever thou turnest thyself" (1 Kings 2:3)

"And they set the priests in their divisions, and the Levites in their courses, for the service of God, which is at Jerusalem; as it is written in the book of Moses" (Ezra 6:18)

"Yea, all Israel have transgressed thy law, even by departing, that they might not obey thy voice; therefore the curse is poured upon us, and the oath that is written in the law of

How the Bible Came To Us

Moses the servant of God, because we have sinned against him. And he hath confirmed his words, which he spake against us, and against our judges that judged us, by bringing upon us a great evil: for under the whole heaven hath not been done as hath been done upon Jerusalem. As it is written in the law of Moses, all this evil is come upon us: yet made we not our prayer before the LORD our God, that we might turn from our iniquities, and understand thy truth" (Daniel 9:11-13)

"Remember ye the law of Moses my servant, which I commanded unto him in Horeb for all Israel, with the statutes and judgments" (Malachi 4:4)

Few New Testament verses quoting Moses as the writer of Pentateuch are quoted here.

He saith unto them, Moses because of the hardness of your hearts suffered you to put away your wives: but from the beginning it was not so. (Matthew 19:8)

And as touching the dead, that they rise: have ye not read in the book of Moses, how in the bush God spake unto him, saying, I am the God of Abraham, and the God of Isaac, and the God of Jacob? (Mark 12:26)

For Moses describeth the righteousness which is of the law, That the man which doeth those things shall live by them. (Romans 10:5)

"For had ye believed Moses, ye would have believed me: for he wrote of me" (John 5:46)

Although there are evidences from other historians, yet I will quote two evidences about Moses and his writings from Jewish Historian Flavius Joseph. As this suffices the need to understand

How the Bible Came To Us

that Moses lived during in Egypt during time when Pharaoh persecuted the children of Israel, and he, by the hand of God, led them from Egypt to up to the borders of Canaan, and also that he wrote the Pentateuch, I hope not to dwell more on proving that Moses wrote Pentateuch (Torah).

"When Moses had thus addressed himself to God, he smote the sea with his rod, which parted asunder at the stroke, and receiving those waters into itself, left the ground dry, as a road and a place of flight for the Hebrews"[9]

"Moses also wrote their blessings and their curses, that they might learn them so thoroughly, that they might never be forgotten by length of time..."[10]

---

[9] *Flavius Joseph Antiquities of the Jews – 02 Chapter 16 Para 2*

[10] *Flavius Joseph Book 04 Chapter 8 Para 44.*

How the Bible Came To Us

CHAPTER 8
MASORETES AND MASORETIC TEXT

EARLY SCRIPT AND TANAKH

"Masoretic Text" is the authorized text of Hebrew Text used in "Tanakh".

"Masorah" is "a collection of critical and explanatory notes on the Hebrew text of the Old Testament, compiled from the 7th? to 10th centuries a.d. and traditionally accepted as an authoritative exegetic guide, chiefly in matters of pronunciation and grammar" (Dictionary)

"Masorete" is one of the writers or compilers of the Masorah (Dictionary)

Scholars from Talmudic Academies of Babylonia and Palestine, who undertook the project of codifying meticulously by providing diacritical marks in order to pronounce the words correctly, were "Masoretes" and their project was called "Masoretic Text".

The Masoretic Text which was used to write the Hebrew Bible was given the status of being considered as the "original text". Their venture was of no small significance inasmuch as they made sure that the Hebrew Bible had the original text gathered from the fragments of manuscripts available to them. This Hebrew Bible was their "Tanakh" which enjoyed invincible patronage of Jews for over six hundred years. Their effort was to transmit the pure words of God to the future generations.

"The words of the LORD are pure words: as silver tried in a furnace of earth, purified seven times" (Psalms 12:6)

How the Bible Came To Us

Every word and every letter of the Masoretic Text was the product of their meticulous checking and taking care of the unusual grammar, correcting discrepancies and spellings etc. of the various texts they had with them. They filled the vacuum in the original script that had no vowels in them by introducing vowels to ensure that they words in the sentences are pronounced correctly and this undoubtedly helped the Hebrew Bible to be read with much ease in their synagogues.

The Masoretes were meticulous in making sure that they did not leave out any text, and when the final codification of each section was complete they counted the number of verses, words, and letters in the text and in addition that also indicated which letter marks the center of the text in a verse. The remarkable consistency it had rendered credibility to the text and it obviously enjoyed the undeniable patronage of Jews for over six hundred years. It was their Hebrew Bible, which was also called Tanakh.

"Palaeography (UK) or paleography (US; ultimately from Greek: παλαιός, palaiós, "old", and γράφειν, graphein, "to write") is the study of ancient and historical handwriting (that is to say, of the forms and processes of writing, not the textual content of documents). Included in the discipline is the practice of deciphering, reading, and dating historical manuscripts, and the cultural context of writing, including the methods with which writing and books were produced, and the history of scriptoria"[11].

TANAKH

Tanakh[12] is a compilation of "Torah", "Nevi'im" and "Ketuvim"

---

[11] Wikipedia, n.d. Web[22 Apr, 2015]

How the Bible Came To Us

The word "Torah", if translated into English, it simply means "Instruction". It is the Law given by God, and consists of oral Law and written law of God. This Law existed before the foundations of the world in heavens, and God gave to the children of Israel this Law by the hand of Moses, the servant of God. The Oral instructions existed many years before the written Law came into existence. God's word was initially given in the form of "Oral Law", which was transmitted down the ages from father to son and teacher to student. It is the way God, initially, communed with Adam, Eve, Cain and others up until the "Ten Commandments" were given on the Mount Sinai to Moses. Later, God spoke to men in different ways.

"Torah" now refers to the Jewish Sacred Text, also called Hebrew Bible used by the followers of "Judaism", which is "the monotheistic religion of the Jews, tracing its origins to Abraham and having its spiritual and ethical principles embodied chiefly in the Hebrew Scriptures and the Talmud" (Definition from dictionary).

"Torah is also called "Pentateuch[13]" in the Holy Bible, and consists of the same books as in "Torah".

These five books are Genesis, Exodus, Leviticus, Numbers and Deuteronomy and same as Jewish Torah, except for presentation of text in certain passages, for example, the letter "O" is not written in the word "God". The word is written as "G_d" in Jewish texts, because they believe God's name should not be taken in vain. "YHWH" is Yahweh; however while speaking they call God as "Adonai". Christians are indebted to

---

[12] Wikipedia, n.d. Web [22 Apr, 2015]

[13] Wiener, Harold M. International Standard Bible Encyclopedia, n.d. Web[22 Apr, 2015]

How the Bible Came To Us

Jews because it is they who preserved the sacred texts and the Pentateuch is adapted as the first five Books by Christians.

"Nevi'im" consists of Seven Major Prophets, and Twelve Minor Prophets

"Ketuvim" consists of writings in eleven books written by various individuals

Although the books in the "Tanakh" and the "Old Testament" are same, yet the term "Old Testament" cannot be attributed to Jewish Sacred Text "Tanakh". The Terms "Tanakh" and "Ketuvim" are exclusively used in "Judaism".

Christians have only Two Books distinguished as "Old Testament" and the "New Testament". The Old Testament contains thirty nine books and the New Testament contains twenty seven books. The Two Testaments together is called the "Bible", which is the sacred Scripture for Christians.

CHAPTER 9
SEPTUAGINT

(Septuagint[14] is often referred to in Roman Numerals as LXX)

BACKGROUND

"And when he shall stand up, his kingdom shall be broken, and shall be divided toward the four winds of heaven; and not to his posterity, nor according to his dominion which he ruled: for his kingdom shall be plucked up, even for others beside those" (Daniel 11:4)

Alexander was the son of Philip of Macedon. He was born in 356 BC and reigned from 332-323BC. It was because he conquered many kingdoms he was given the title "the Great" as suffix to his name, and thus he was called "Alexander the Great".

Philip was killed when Alexander was twenty year old man. Alexander the great conquered Persia in 331 B.C. and thus Jews, who were under his regime, adopted Greek culture, and were called "Hellenists". Greek Language became very popular rendering Hebrew Language almost into redundancy.

Inasmuch as Alexander the great did not leave behind any "will" as to who would inherit his throne, there was commotion among the four generals, who were in-charge of four regions, under his regime. The kingdom was divided into four "as four winds of heaven", and the four generals took a region each. (cf. Daniel 8:21-22; Daniel 11:3-4).

---

[14] (1) "Alexander, the Great, n.d. International Standard Bible Encyclopedia. Web[06 May 2015]
(2) "Septuagint" Wikipedia n.d. Web [05 May, 2015]

How the Bible Came To Us

Alexander the great had already established two kingdoms known as Kingdom of Ptolemy and Kingdom of Seleucids, who subsequently fought with each other until the onset of Maccabean War in 165 B.C. The result was an emergence of common Jewish Kingdom that lasted for about one hundred years eventually paving the way for Greek Language to flourish in Alexandria, which was in Egypt.

Under Ptolemy II (Philadelphus [285-246 BC]) Jews were allowed to build synagogues to worship their God. The King ordered translation of Jewish Scriptures (Hebrew Bible which we identify as the "Old Testament") into Greek Language, initially for his library, and it eventually became the most authoritative scripture among Jews and Christians.

THE SEVENTY

It was during that time that seventy or seventy two scholars translated into Greek language the Hebrew Scriptures, which Jews call as "Hebrew Bible" and Christians as the "Old Testament". This is not to be confused with "Mazorites text", which was authoritative Hebrew Text of "Tanakh", compiled by several Hebrew Scholars from the original Hebrew Scriptures, from sixth to tenth centuries. "Septuagint" in Latin simply means the "seventy".

From the last days of the prophet Malachi until the commencement of the ministry of Lord Jesus Christ there was a silence for about four hundred years, during which time some dubious and spurious documents came up purportedly as inspired texts called apocryphal books, which were included only for historical reasons in Septuagint, along with thirty nine books.

How the Bible Came To Us

Scholars, after careful study, set aside those "apocryphal books" before the Bible was canonized, primarily because the New Testament writers never quoted any writing from "apocrypha", a name that was coined by Latin Scholar St. Jerome who translated in 4 Century A.D., the Bible into "vulgate", which is the Latin version of the Bible and "used as the authorized version of the Roman Catholic Church[15]"

Christians derived great help from the Septuagint while proclaiming the Gospel of Lord Jesus Christ to Jews and Gentiles during the early years, after the ascension of Jesus, because most of the Jews spoke Greek by then.

It was a time when Jewish Maccabean kingdom was conquered by the Roman Government and thus the Greek became a dominant language for communication. Evangelists were comfortable in citing the New Testament references from the Old Testament, and thus proving that Jesus was spoken of in the Old Testament.

Many quotes from the Hebrew Bible are taken from the Septuagint and compared with the writings in the Gospels and Epistles thus proving that Jesus came not to abolish the Law of Moses, but to fulfill the Moses Law.

When the Mazorites text and Septuagint was compared there were few differences, but they were not worth of any cognizance. The fundamental doctrines and the deity of Lord Jesus Christ were never compromised even with the presence of minor errors either in the translation or in spelling. The Old Testament Prophecies that were in the Septuagint, and in the Dead Sea Scrolls, were amazingly found to have been pre-dated

---

[15] Dictionary

How the Bible Came To Us

the birth of Lord Jesus, and thus establishing perfect evidence that Jesus was the Messiah to come.

Psalm 22 and Isaiah 53 are indelible evidences of Christ's sufferings for the sake of man in order to redeem man from his sin. The salvation is available free of cost for all those who acknowledge Jesus as the Lord and believe in heart that God raised Him from the dead (Romans 10:9-10)

How the Bible Came To Us

CHAPTER 10
SCRIPTURES AND SCROLLS

"That saith of Cyrus, He is my shepherd, and shall perform all my pleasure: even saying to Jerusalem, Thou shalt be built; and to the temple, Thy foundation shall be laid" (Isaiah 44:28)

God spoke through Isaiah 700 B.C., about what was going to happen to the children of Israel in one hundred years from then. It was about the captivity of Jews by Nebuchadnezzar, the king of Babylon. In circa 600 B.C. the Jews were taken captive by the Babylonian king. However, the Lord also gave them the promise that after disciplining them He will bring them back to their land. In 538 B.C., all the willing children of Israel returned to Israel in three phases.

God knows future, and knows what He was going to do. He said their physical redeemer was going to 160 years later, who will subdue Babylonians and many other kingdoms as well. God through Isaiah the prophet named their redeemer and it was King Cyrus who came as their redeemer.

The first Chapter of the Book of Ezra contains the details of the orders given by Cyrus, the king of Persia, according to the Word of the LORD, to build the house of the LORD God of Israel (cf. Jeremiah 25:12-14; 29:10; 33:7-13; Daniel 9:1-27; Isaiah 44:28; Esther 1:1-3).

In addition to Biblical evidences of scriptures written in Hebrew, Aramaic, and Greek there are historical evidences as to the languages used in the scriptures.

How the Bible Came To Us

Flavius Joseph, Jewish historian wrote about "the captivity of the Ten Tribes to the first year of Cyrus" in his Antiquities of the Jews – Book 10 Chapters 1 to 11

All this and more that were written on seven scrolls known as "Dead Sea Scrolls" were discovered in Qumran cave in 1947. The scroll of Isaiah had sixty six books that were written in Hebrew. The Old Testament was mostly written in Hebrew, except for few chapters in Ezra and Daniel and a verse in Jeremiah was written in Aramaic. Moses was the first author to write in Hebrew script and he wrote the "Torah".

Biblical scholars used the term "Hebrew Bible" to refer to "Tanakh", the collection of Jewish texts[16]. The Tanakh contains…

Torah with first five books namely Genesis, Exodus, Leviticus, Numbers and Deuteronomy

Nevi'im with Seven Major Prophets (Samuel and Kings are counted as two instead of four) and twelve Minor Prophets and they are…

Major Prophets:

Joshua, Judges, Samuel, Kings, Isaiah, Jeremiah, and Ezekiel

Minor Prophets:

Hosea, Joel, Amos, Obadiah, Jonah, Micah, Nahum, Habakkuk, Zephaniah, Haggai, Zechariah, and Malachi

Ketuvim with writings of various individuals namely

---

[16] "Hebrew Bible" Wikipedia, n.d. Web [3 May, 2015]

How the Bible Came To Us

Three poetic books viz., Psalms, Proverbs, and Job

Five Scrolls viz., Song of Songs, Ruth, Lamentations, Ecclesiastes, and Esther

Other books viz., Daniel, Ezra, Nehemiah and Chronicles

The manuscripts of the Hebrew Bible and the Dead Sea Scrolls are believed to have been written in 2nd Century and the Greek translation of the Hebrew Bible called "Septuagint[17]" (abbreviated as LXX), which had its origin in Alexandria, was written between 300-200 BC. About seventy scholars, commissioned by Ptolemy translated Jewish Bible from Hebrew to Greek, and the text is so named after their number, the seventy or "Septuagint". The Septuagint contains not only thirty nine books of the Tanakh, but also Apocryphal books.

Apocryphal books were good for historical reasons and to have knowledge about Christianity and various books and the dates of the books, but they are not recognized as inspired Scriptures to be included in the Christian Bible. Biblical Scholar Jerome coined the word "Apocrypha" and books viz., Maccabees are very useful for information.

While Roman Catholic Church and Orthodox churches included Apocrypha the Protestant Church did not recognize Apocryphal books as inspired books and, therefore, the Bible does not contain Apocryphal books.

---

[17] "Septuagint" All About GOD Ministries, n.d. Web, [03 May, 2015]

How the Bible Came To Us

CHAPTER 11
NEW TESTAMENT AND THE LANGUAGE

A Testament is a will or covenant made to come into effect after the death of the person making the testament.

The New Testament has come into effect after the death, burial and Resurrection of Lord Jesus Christ. The New Testament deals with the birth of Lord Jesus Christ, His works, His teachings, His death, burial, His Resurrection and ascension. The New Testament also deals with the eschatology, which is about the second coming of Lord Jesus Christ, His millennial rule, and eternity.

After the ascension of Lord Jesus Christ the Father has sent Holy Spirit into this world to guide, convict the believers in Christ.

Old Covenant deals with Abrahamic Covenant, Mosaic Law, the prophets, Biblical History, Biblical poems and other Hebrew scriptures written by many Godly persons inspired by God. The appropriate title of the Old Testament, therefore, could be "Hebrew Scriptures" or "Tanakh". The title "Old Testament", in my opinion, is relevant only in the light of the title "New Testament", because Old Testament is not old and it still is alive not only for Jews, but also for Christians. The New Testament in itself is already two thousand years old now.

It is therefore important for Christians to consider the Holy Bible in its entirety as Inspired Holy Scriptures of the Living God, rather than separating the Bible as Old and New Testaments. For the purpose of identification and not to confuse we will still identify the books in the Old Testament as Old Testament

How the Bible Came To Us

Books, and the books, epistles, and Apocalypse (The Book of Revelation) as the New Testament. A very important point to be borne in mind is that New Testament deals mainly with Lord Jesus Christ and His teachings. They are elaborated by Apostle Paul, and other disciples of Lord Jesus Christ, as guided by the Holy Spirit.

Knowledge in the Hebrew language, Aramaic, and Greek is an added advantage for Christians inasmuch as the need to refer to the words and the context where the verses appear becomes imperative in cases of disputed interpretations of the scriptures.

New Testament is written in Koine Greek[18], and later translated into many languages of the world. Koine Greek was the mainstream language when Alexander the Great ruled Eastern Mediterranean region from (335-323 BC) until Byzantine Greek (Medieval Greek)[19] became popular in Circa 600 BC) The word "Canon" means "the body of rules, principles, or standards accepted as axiomatic and universally binding in a field of study or art".

The Bible was canonized and it is decided that the Holy Scriptures in the Bible should have only thirty nine books in the Old Testament and twenty seven books in the New Testament. There are Apocryphal books containing very useful information and history, but they are not included in the Bible.

The inclusion of several books, epistles, Apocalypse and deletion of apocryphal books is not done with the human wisdom or according to human preferences, but with exclusive

---

[18] Kurt Aland, Barbara Aland The text of the New Testament: an introduction to the critical 1995 p52

[19] "Byzantine Greek" (Medieval Greek), Wikipedia, n.d. [22 Apr, 2015]

How the Bible Came To Us

guidance by God through Holy Spirit and, therefore, only God's inspired Scriptures are included in the Bible.

How the Bible Came To Us

A NEW TESTAMENT FRAGMENT

Any handwritten copy of a portion of the text of the Bible is a "biblical manuscript". The word "Bible" is a derivative of the Greek Word *"biblia"*, which means "books". The canonized Bible Protestants use is made up of sixty six books.

A copy of a portion of the New Testament made on "Papyrus" is called a "New Testament Papyrus. There are over one hundred and twenty papyri which in general stand out as the earliest witnesses.

One such papyrus, of several papyri, is presented here to give a general idea.

NEW TESTAMENT PAPYRI [20]

The Greek text-type of this codex is a representative of the Alexandrian. Aland placed it in Category I.[21]

Matthew 1:1-9, 12, 14-20[22]

Scholars identified 𝔓1 as the closest in agreement with the Codex Vaticanus.

Text according to Comfort
Recto

---

[20] "List of New Testament papyri" Wikipedia n.d. web [30 May 2015]
[21] Aland, Kurt; Aland, Barbara (1995). The Text of the New Testament: An Introduction to the Critical Editions and to the Theory and Practice of Modern Textual Criticism. Erroll F. Rhodes (trans.). Grand Rapids: William B. Eerdmans Publishing Company. p. 96. ISBN 978-0-8028-4098-1
[22] http://ntvmr.uni-muenster.de/manuscript-workspace/?docID=10001

How the Bible Came To Us

α
[1:1] βιβλος γενεσεως ΙΥ ΧΥ ΥΥ δαυιδ [ΥΥ]
αβρααμ [1:2] αβρααμ εγεννησεν τον [ισαακ]
ισαακ δ[ε] εγεννησεν τ[ον] ιακωβ [ιακωβ]
δε εγ[ε]ννησεν τον ιουδαν κ[α]ι τ[ους]
α[δ]ελφους αυτου [1:3] ιουδας δε εγεννη
σεν τον φαρες και τον ζαρε εκ της θα
μαρ φαρες δε εγεννησεν τον εσρωμ
εσ[ρω]μ δε εγεννησεν τ[ο]ν αραμ [1:4] α[ραμ]
δε [ε]γεννησεν τον αμμιναδαβ αμ
μ[ι]ναδ[α]β δε εγεννησεν τον ναασσων
ναα[σ]σων δε εγενν[ησ]εν τον σαλ[μω]ν
[1:5] σαλμων δε εγενν[η]σεν τον βοες [εκ]
της ραχαβ βοες δε εγεννησεν τον ι
ωβηδ εκ της ρ[ο]υθ ιω[βηδ δ]ε εγεννη
σεν τον ιεσσαι [1:6] ιεσσ[αι] δε εγεννησεν
τον δαυιδ τον βασιλε[α δαυ]ιδ δε εγεν
νησεν τον σολομωνα εκ της ουρειου. [1:7] σο
λομων δε εγεννησεν τον [ρ]οβοαμ ροβο
αμ δε εγεννησεν τ[ο]ν [αβει]α αβεια δε
εγεννησεν [το]ν ασα[φ] [1:8] [α]σ[α]φ δε εγεν
νησεν τον ιωσαφατ ι[ω]σαφατ δ[ε] εγεν
ν[η]σε[ν] τον ιωραμ ιωραμ δε εγεν[νησεν
τον] οζε[ι]αν [1:9] οζειας δε εγεν[νησεν]
lacuna [1:12] lacuna [με
τοικεσιαν βαβυλωνος ιεχονι]ας εγ[εν
νησεν] lacuna

How the Bible Came To Us

[23]Copyright information

Verso
[1:14] [lacuna] β
[τον σ]αδω[κ σ]αδωκ δε εγεννησεν το[ν
αχειμ] αχειμ δε εγε[ν]νησεν τον ελιου[δ]
[1:15] [ελιου]δ δε εγ[εν]νη[σ]ε[ν] τον ελεαζαρ ελε
[αζ]αρ [δε εγ]εννησεν [το]ν μαθθαν μαθθα[ν]
δε εγεννη[σ]εν τον [ι]ακωβ [1:16] ιακωβ δε
[εγ]εννησεν τον ιωσηφ τον ανδρα μ[α]
ριας [ε]ξ ης εγενν[ηθ]η ΙΣ ο λεγομενο[ς ΧΣ]
[1:17] πασαι ουν γε[νε]αι απο αβρααμ εως
δαυιδ γενεαι ΙΔ και απο [δ]α[υ]ιδ [ε]ως τη[ς]
μετοικεσιας βαβυλωνο[ς] γε[νεαι] ΙΔ κα[ι]
απο της μετ[οι]κεσιας βαβ[υ]λων[ο]ς εως
του ΧΥ γενεαι [Ι]Δ [1:18] του δε ΙΥ ΧΥ η γενε
σις ουτως ην μνηστε[υ]θεισης της μη
τρος αυτου μ[αρι]α[ς] τω [ιω]σηφ πριν η συν
[ε]λθε[ι]ν αυ[το]υ[ς] ευρε[θη] εν γαστρι εχου
σα ε[κ ΠΝΣ αγιου] [1:19] [ιωσηφ δε ο] ανηρ αυ
της [δι]και[ος ων και μη θελων αυτην]
δειγμα[τ]ε[ισαι εβουλη]θη [λαθρα
α]πολυ[σαι] α[υ]τ[η]ν [1:20] [τ]αυτα [δε αυτου εν
θ]υμη[θεντος ι]δου αγ[γελο]ς ΚΥ [κ]α[τ
ο]ναρ [εφανη αυ]τω [λεγων] ιωσ[η]φ

---

[23] http://creativecommons.org/licenses/by-sa/3.0/deed.en_US { { PD-US} }

How the Bible Came To Us

υιος] δ[αυιδ] μ[η] φο[βηθη]ς παρ[αλαβ]ει

[μ]αριαν [την] γυναι[κα σου] το [γαρ εν αυ

τη γεν]νηθεν ε[κ] ΠΝΣ [εστιν] α[γιου]

[1:21-23] lacuna

με[θερμηνευομενον μεθ ημων ο ΘΣ]

Disagreement with Vaticanus (according to Hoskier[24])

Papyrus 1	Vaticanus
ΥΥ	ΥΙΟΥ
ΔΑΥΙΔ	ΔΑΥΕΙΔ
ΑΜΙΝΑΔΑΒ	
ΔΑΥΙΔ	ΑΜΕΙΝΑΔΑΒ
ΤΗΣ ΟΥΡΕΙΟΥ	ΔΑΥΕΙΔ
ΑΒ[ΕΙ]Α	ΤΗΣ ΤΟΥ ΟΥΡΕΙΟΥ
ΑΒΕΙΑ	ΑΒΙΑ
ΕΓΕ[ΝΗΣΕΝ]	ΑΒΙΑ
illeg	ΓΕΝΝΑ
illeg	ΤΟΝ ΣΕΛΑΘΙΗΛ
illeg	ΣΕΛΑΘΙΗΛ ΔΕ ΓΕΝΝΑ
ΜΑΘΘΑΝ	ΑΒΙΟΥΤ
ΙΩΣΗΦ	ΜΑΤΘΑΝ
ΓΕΝΕΑΙ	ΤΟΝ ΙΩΣΗΦ
ΔΑΥΙΔ	ΑΙ ΓΕΝΕΑΙ
ΔΑΥΙΔ	ΔΑΥΕΙΔ
ΙΔ	ΔΑΥΕΙΔ
ΙΥ ΧΥ	ΔΕΚΑΤΕΣΣΑΡΕΣ
ΔΕΙΓΜΑ[Τ]ΕΙΣΑΙ	ΧΥ ΙΥ
ΔΑΥΙΔ	ΔΕΙΓΜΑΤΙΣΑΙ
	ΔΑΥΕΙΔ[6]

----

[24] Hoskier, Codex B and Its Allies, a study and an indictment, Bernard Quaritch (London 1914), p. XI

CHAPTER 12
GOD SPOKE THROUGH PROPHETS

The LORD spoke future events through the prophets and when they spoke they said "thus says the LORD", not knowing what they were speaking about the future. Prophetic utterances had two implications; one of fulfillment immediately and the other way too many years later. Tracing back fulfilment of prophecies from New Testament to the Old Testament show how accurately prophets spoke. There are thousands of prophecies about Lord Jesus Christ that are fulfilled in the New Testament period exactly as they were prophesied.

There are prophecies of eschatology (that is, of the end days), which will surely come to pass. Lord Jesus Christ said

"Heaven and earth will pass away, but my words will not pass away" (Mark 13:31 ESV; also cf. Psalm 102:26; Isaiah 51:6; 2 Peter 3:10; Matthew 5:18)

None of the prophets, except Lord Jesus Christ, who was the head of the Church, prophet, priest and King of kings, and Lord of lords, none of the prophets(not even Daniel) who spoke prophecies knew what they spoke, but their prophecies are fulfilled and the prophecies of end days will be fulfilled without any failure.

"But thou, O Daniel, shut up the words, and seal the book, even to the time of the end: many shall run to and fro, and knowledge shall be increased. Then I Daniel looked, and, behold, there stood other two, the one on this side of the bank of the river, and the other on that side of the bank of the river. And one said to the man clothed in linen, which was upon the

How the Bible Came To Us

waters of the river, How long shall it be to the end of these wonders? And I heard the man clothed in linen, which was upon the waters of the river, when he held up his right hand and his left hand unto heaven, and sware by him that liveth for ever that it shall be for a time, times, and an half; and when he shall have accomplished to scatter the power of the holy people, all these things shall be finished. And I heard, but I understood not: then said I, O my Lord, what shall be the end of these things? And he said, Go thy way, Daniel: for the words are closed up and sealed till the time of the end" (Daniel 12:4-9).

Apostle Peter infuses confidence and restores confidence in the minds of Jews scattered among nations, after they suffered persecutions in the early days of Christianity that they should rejoice in the Lord. His admonition is also applicable to the Gentiles who were in various nations (cf. 1 Peter 1:18, 2:10, 4:3)

"Which in time past were not a people, but are now the people of God: which had not obtained mercy, but now have obtained mercy" (1 Peter 2:10).

Peter spoke of the bright future that every child of God will enjoy even though the present day trials are manifold. His usage of the word "precious" several times is quite noticeable and obvious. He says, the trial of their faith was greater in value than that of gold that perishes.

Was it impossible for God to provide written script for Adam and Eve? No, but that was not in the plan of God. God spoke to man in different ways in different periods of time. He spoke probably by His physical appearance to Adam and Eve (Gen.2:16), by His voice to Adam (3:8), and to Moses from the burning bush (Exo.3:4), by Urim and Thummim to the high priest in the Tabernacle (cf. Exo. 28:30), to Hannah by Prophet

How the Bible Came To Us

Eli (1:17); warned the children of Israel by the mouth of several prophets, and in the last days He spoke by His only son Lord Jesus Christ.

In the meanwhile, God provided scripts in different forms; the Ten Commandments by His own fingers (Deut. 9:10), by providing material called "Papyrus" made out of plant by the side of Nile river in Egypt, where mother of Moses used the said plant for hiding him in a basket made out of Papyrus. As the time passed God's word passed on vellum, parchments, paper for us to read and be edified. Every believer had the Word of God in the manner the LORD provided for them and they all believed and gained everlasting life.

It is for the people of God in the Church to read and understand the things that God planned many years before that in due season the script is made available in advance format. In the present age the Gospel of John speaks it all. The culmination of all shadows and ante-types ended in the substance in Lord Jesus Christ, who is the only mediator and the high priest and none can reach or speak to the Father in heaven except by Him and Him alone.

The prophets prophesied of the grace that was to come to them, and searched as to the time-phase such grace period would come. They did not speak for themselves, but they spoke for those who were there then, and received preaching with the help of Holy Spirit. Even angels desired to know of that salvation by grace through faith would come about. (cf. 1 Peter 1:10-13)

"Of which salvation the prophets have enquired and searched diligently, who prophesied of the grace that should come unto you: Searching what, or what manner of time the Spirit of Christ which was in them did signify, when it testified beforehand the sufferings of Christ, and the glory that should follow. Unto whom it was revealed, that not unto themselves, but unto us they did minister the things, which are now reported unto you by them that have preached the gospel unto you with the Holy Ghost sent down from heaven; which things the angels desire to look into" (1 Peter 1:10-12).

How the Bible Came To Us

CHAPTER 13
TEXTUAL CRITICISM

Textual criticism[25] is positive criticism in order to search for the clues that determine the text that was to be included, and the text that was to be deleted from the documents found as a result of researches to compile the text, as close to the original text that was written in Hebrew, Aramaic, and Greek languages, as possible. Unless extreme care was taken under the guidance of Holy Spirit we would not have received the final inerrant Bible that we have now.

The Text in the original languages was not found in one place or in one book, but was found in various places either as loose papyrus leaflets, or parched scrolls made of animal skin on which the text was inscribed, or as scrolls containing various sheets stitched together.

The history played major role in the scattering of the originally written material whereon the text was written. Earthquakes, tornadoes, hurricanes, and wars would have all contributed to the scattering of the Holy Scriptures written by the original authors. They were all scattered from the time of Moses, who wrote "Torah" in Hebrew, and the rest of the books by prophets and others in Hebrew and Aramaic languages and apostolic writings.

Researchers, who undertook the task of gathering the papyrus scrolls, and other material with God's out-breathed words

---

[25] 1. The study of manuscripts or printings to determine the original or most authoritative form of a text, especially of a piece of literature.
2. Literary criticism stressing close reading and detailed analysis of a particular text.

How the Bible Came To Us

written on them, found the scriptures in the buried soil or scattered around

After few centuries from the time the texts were found by the researchers, scholars who undertook the task of putting together these pieces of information into one book, had tough time doing their job under the guidance of God spanning many years.

The collection of such documents ranged from the period of Moses the servant of God to the period of Apostles and the documents subjected to severe positive criticism to correct the errors in order to emulate the final text as much close to the original documents of Old Testament and the writings of apostles as possible.

It is not within the scope of this article/book to go into the details of the discussion as to how many errors have occurred in translating the original text and how much change has occurred in printing the copied text. Inasmuch as it is a vast subject and that there are already many articles out there specifying the details as to how original text in some verses is missing or some additions were made to the original writings inadvertently, or sometimes even deliberately, not with any bad intention of exalting Christianity over others, but to match with the truth of the Deity of Lord Jesus Christ and Triune God, any writing by me pointing the individual errors, as if I did research, would be superfluous.

The subject matter for consideration now is how the text came to us as we read it in the Bible today. There are few who say Bible contains errors and there are those who say the text is not the same as God spoke to His people. Much of it depends on as to how a man believes in God; and unless God takes exceptional

How the Bible Came To Us

interest in a man who is out there to contradict anything or everything written in the Bible, no one can help the man who has decided to rebel against God.

"Textus Receptus" was the text received from the period of Reformation to that of post-reformation era and the other is of the Greek text from B.F. Westcott and F.J.A Hort, who did great dedicated research over a period of twenty eight years. While publishing the second edition of the Greek text of the New Testament almost after one hundred and twenty years the publishers quipped "therefore you have the text now received by all," and the text thus received was called "Textus Receptus[26]" that had large amount of text from Erasmus

In spite of great care taken over many years, minor crept into various translations. None of such variations were intentionally done, albeit textual criticism was done by humans, and therefore, the weakness of human element of understanding the text was alive.

Nevertheless, as the scriptures were inspired by God the theme did not miss the mark. The reader should give credence to the task that was carried out of elaborate copying process and printing of the text from sixty six books from various languages to finalize the text for canonization of the greatest book in the world, the "Bible".

If one has positive thinking one will see Lord Jesus meeting him in the Word. Several dedicated God's servants made attempts to bring the text as close to the originals as possible. Even

---

[26] See *He Kaine Diatheke: The New Testament. The Greek text underlying the English Authorized Version of 1611* (London: Trinitarian Bible Society, 1980), "preface."

How the Bible Came To Us

though the differences found from the researches are insignificant, probably of one hundred minor variations or so, Christians tend to debate over this issue vehemently frittering away time and energy.

The Scholars tried their best to put the things in order; however it is true that no one is beyond the human limitations. It is hard to conclude that the writers were inspired, rather than the Scriptures. God breathed His Spirit into the words of the Bible and His Word lasts.

Neither Westcott and Hort, nor Textus Receptus or Erasmus or Nestle or Hodges was omniscient or perfect in reasoning and judgment. We are all human beings. We all depend on Holy Spirit's Guidance. Whenever there is a dispute on interpretation it is imperative that we consult the Lexicons containing words and meanings of original language and prayerfully come to conclusion as guided by the Holy Spirit and see Lord Jesus Christ in the Scriptures.

TEXTUS RECEPTUS
ERASMUS TEXT: LAST PAGE
REV22 8 21.jpg[27]

---

[27] {{PD-US}} – published in the US before 1923 and public domain in the US.

CHAPTER 14
THE LIFE OF JESUS

Lord Jesus Christ lived for thirty three and half years on this earth during the period when Roman Government had control over Israel. During His ministry on this earth he left behind several witnesses of His works, His ministry, His death, His burial, His resurrection and His ascension. The witnesses included His disciples, His followers, and Roman Government officials like Pilate, Herod, Nicodemus, and Joseph of Arimathea. Nicodemus was a ruler of Jews and Joseph of Arimathea was a councilor of honorable estate and a member of Sanhedrin. In addition, there were many who were healed by His miracles witnessed about Him.

Therefore, the question of His existence or His ministry, and His miraculous works, His death by His crucifixion, His burial in the new tomb of Joseph of Arimathea, the empty tomb, His appearance to many for forty days of His resurrection are as true as the day is day, and the night is night. If one believes that darkness looms large when there is no light, then it is true that light is not darkness just as darkness is not light and such is the truth about the Lord Jesus Christ's death, burial and His resurrection from the dead.

There were historians and scientists who recorded as to what happened on this earth of the things that have occurred millions of years ago. The greatest truth is that God is eternal and He was before the world was. He spoke to men in diverse ways and in the last days He spoke through His one and only Son Lord Jesus Christ lived, who in His incarnation did not think it to be robbery to be with the Father but relinquished His glory with

How the Bible Came To Us

the Father and came down to this earth in the form of servant and in the likeness of man. He lived among men and men did not know that He was the light. His works and the events of His life were recorded within one hundred years after His ascension.

Three synoptic Gospels, Matthew, Mark and Luke, and the fourth one the Gospel of John were written by four different individuals and yet they all speak about the glorious works of Lord Jesus Christ. That was how Holy Spirit guided them to write the Gospels. Also there were epistles written by Apostle Paul and other disciples of Jesus Christ. The most important book in the Bible is Revelation which also called Apocalypse speaks of the future. Scripture corroborates scripture and that was How God helped His servants to knit the thoughts of God and His message to men in one great book called the "Bible".

It is not worth making big deal on the dates they were written, and the way they were presented as long as the essence of the life of Lord Jesus Christ, His works, His death, burial, Resurrection and Ascension are indisputable. If one cannot disprove Jesus's death on the cross, His burial, His Resurrection and Ascension, then one should believe based on the verifiable records available.

Matthew and John were disciples of Jesus. Mark was a friend of Apostle Paul, and Luke a physician, who accompanied Paul in his missionary journeys. They all died before AD 100 and, therefore, it is evident that the entire New Testament was written during their life time before AD 100.

How the Bible Came To Us

CHAPTER 15
THE CODICES

"Heaven and earth shall pass away, but my words shall not pass away" (Matthew 24:35)

God's in His providence and love toward men made available to men, after many years, the oldest manuscripts of various writers who built the text upon the original writings of the inspired writers, like Moses and other prophets, and apostles, who wrote God's Word in Hebrew, Aramaic, and Greek. The originals written by them were called "autographs" which are not available today. What are available today are copies of copies of these "autographs".

Inspired men of God recorded God's Word by hand on papyri and parchments, fragments of which were found many years later. These fragments contained God's Word and His communication with men, in different ages and, in different forms. The LORD spoke to men in various ways in different ages. He spoke through prophets; He spoke in audible voice, He spoke in the hearts of believers, and in the last days He spoke through His Son Lord Jesus Christ.

Prophet Isaiah wrote…

"Lift up your eyes to the heavens, and look upon the earth beneath: for the heavens shall vanish away like smoke, and the earth shall wax old like a garment, and they that dwell therein shall die in like manner: but my salvation shall be for ever, and my righteousness shall not be abolished" (Isaiah 51:6)

How the Bible Came To Us

AN IMPORTANT YEAR

AD 1454 is an important year. It was in this year that printing press was invented by Johannes Gutenberg, a German blacksmith. Until such time as printing was done by machine there were only manuscripts and it was the only way to copy the text whenever the need arose to duplicate the work which, indeed, was an arduous task, and therefore, seldom an extra copy was made.

As soon as the printing press was invented great interest grew in Godly men, who by their inspiration translated the Biblical text into many languages and printed and distributed copies. The earliest scripture in Europe was in Latin, a language which was not understood by many.

How the Bible Came To Us

Gutenberg Bible[28] in Public Domain Resized to 1500pxx1200px and reused by Leslie John

Licensed under. https://creativecommons.org/licenses/by-sa/2.0/

Quote: The Gutenberg Bible [Bible, Latin Vulgate. Ca. 1455]. Biblia Latina. [Mainz: Johann Gutenberg, ca. 1455]. Rare Books Division. From the Lenox Library The first substantial printed book is this royal-folio two-volume Bible, comprising nearly 1,300 pages, printed in Mainz on the central Rhine by Johann Gutenberg (ca. 1390s-1468) in the 1450s. It was probably completed between March 1455 and November of that year, when Gutenberg's bankruptcy deprived him of his printing establishment and the fruits of his achievements. The Bible epitomizes Gutenberg's triumph, arguably the greatest achievement of the second millennium. Forty-eight integral

---

[28] Gutenberg Bible of the New York Public Library. Bought by James Lenox in 1847, it was the first copy to be acquired by a United States citizen.< https://creativecommons.org/licenses/by-sa/2.0/>

How the Bible Came To Us

copies survive, including eleven on vellum. Perhaps some 180 copies were originally produced, including about 45 on vellum. The Lenox copy, on paper, is the first Gutenberg Bible to come to the United States, in 1847. Its arrival is the stuff of romantic national folklore. James Lenox's European agent issued Instructions for New York that the officers at the Customs House were to remove their hats on seeing it: the privilege of viewing a Gutenberg Bible is vouchsafed to few. (Shortened text copied from placard seen in the background) Unquote

How the Bible Came To Us

CHAPTER 16
VULGATE BIBLE

Latin version of the Bible was called "Latin Vulgate", which was the first Bible translated by Jerome in fourth century. It was commissioned by the erstwhile Pope for official use by the Roman Catholic Church. This Bible was printed in 1456 which led to stepping up interest in producing more New Testament Bibles in single Greek text.

Protestant reformation began in 1517 when Martin Luther[29] wrote his "95 Theses" and submitted to the Church at Wittenberg in Germany. (Some say he posted the "95 Thesis" on the doors of the Church). He opposed the Catholic Church of their corrupt practices of selling "indulgences", and challenged them to debate the two central beliefs, which are the core beliefs of Apostle Paul. He said men can receive salvation only by faith and not by deeds. This challenge brought in a new history to Christianity.

The easiest method of printing Bibles in many languages was to have a single Greek New Testament[30]. The project managers chose to compare the available evidences of manuscripts and compile a single text. Thus invention of Printing Press helped to get rid of production of manuscripts.

A Catholic cardinal named Ximenes printed the first Greek text in 1514 but his project did not receive approval from the

---

[29] Treu, Martin (2003). *Martin Luther in Wittenberg: a biographical tour.* Wittenberg: Saxon-Anhalt Luther Memorial Foundation. p. 15. ISBN 978-3-9808619-4-6. OCLC 60519808
[30] Greenlee, Scribes, Scrolls, and Scriptures, pp. 44-47

How the Bible Came To Us

erstwhile Pope resulting in failure to get the first New Testament to be marketed.

It helped Erasmus, a Dutch scholar to publish his first edition of New Testament in Greek in 1516.

He was followed by another publisher by name Stephanus (also called Robert Estienne) who published four editions in Greek depending heavily on the text from Erasmus.

Stephanus was ingenious in marking out the text into verse divisions which helped him to become popular among scholars. (Chapter divisions were done in 1205 much before the verse divisions were done Stephen Langston, Archbishop of Canterbury).

Beza, a successor of John Calvin published nine editions relying greatly on Erasmus. KJV 1611 edition was his contribution.

Two brothers namely Elzevir[31] brothers from Holland published seven editions of the Greek text. Their second edition contained famous lines in Latin that read "you have therefore the text now received by all, in which we give nothing altered or corrupted." It is from these lines that the phrase "Textus Receptus" ("Received Text") became the keyword of this text.

The books made by stitching the papyri or parchments were called "Codex" (plural Codices).

The three such big codices were[32]...

---

[31] Scrivener, Novum Testamentum : textus Stephanici A.D. 1550 : accedunt variae lectiones editionum Bezae, Elzeviri, Lachmanni, Tischendorfii, Tregellesii (Cambridge 1877)
[32] Credits to Wikipedia

How the Bible Came To Us

1. CODEX ALEXADRINUS
2. CODEX VATICANUS
3. CODEX SINAITICUS

Codex Alexandrinus was an early copy from 5th Century and it was preserved in the National Library of British Museum[33]. It contained the text majority of which was of the Septuagint and the New Testament.

The codex Alexandrinus has almost complete copy of the Septuagint with 773 vellum folios – 630 of the Old Testament and 143 of the New Testament. It is believed that the place of origin of this codex is Alexandria. The manuscript of this codex and its antiquity extensively helped textual critics in their use.

Except for the loss of ten leaves of the Septuagint three of the total four volumes of the codex contain all the folios. The codex also contains deuterocanonical books and some writings ('Ketuvim' as well). New Testament, which is fourth volume of the codex contains Gospels, Acts of the Apostles, Epistles, 2 Thessalonians, Hebrews, 1 Timothy and Book of Revelation.

The Greek text of the codex represented Byzantine text, although the exact relationship to other known texts is still disputed. The text closely resembles to that of Codex Sinaiticus and to that of St. Athnasius.

Codex Alexandrinus was taken to Constantinople in 1621 by Lucar, a patriarch of Alexandria. It is now housed in Royal Library in British Museum. According to some scholars this manuscript is the "oldest and the best in the world".

---

[33] London, British Library, MS Royal 1. D. V-VIII; Gregory-Aland no. A or 02, Soden δ 4

How the Bible Came To Us

Supplementing the codex with Latin Vulgate helped editorial revision of the text at the time of first council at Nicaea[i].

Codex Vaticanus[34] was a copy from 4th century preserved in the library at Vatican for several years but was hidden from public for nearly four hundred years. In 1889-1890 a facsimile was made and it was considered as greatest of all codices

---

[34] The Vatican, Bibl. Vat., Vat. gr. 1209; no. B or 03 Gregory-Aland, δ 1 von Soden

How the Bible Came To Us

VULGATE
iN PUBLIC DOMAIN
By Anonymous (photo by Adrian Pingstone) (Own work)
[Public domain or Public domain], via Wikimedia Commons
https://creativecommons.org/publicdomain/mark/1.0/deed.en

How the Bible Came To Us

CHAPTER 17
CODEX SINAITICUS

Codex Sinaiticus[35] which was a great witness to New Testament was a copy discovered in 4th century and was kept in the National British Library[36].

Codex Sinaiticus is the Greek Text in book format of the Septuagint. Codex is "a quire of manuscript pages held together by stitching: the earliest form of book, replacing the scrolls and wax tablets of earlier times" and "Sinaiticus" is the name of the codex found at the foot of Mount Sainai. This was the most accepted version by the Christians who spoke Greek. This book had manuscripts which had large number of corrections, ranging from corrections of single letter to that of insertion of whole sentence, making sure that the central theme of the Word of God is not changed, and core doctrines are not compromised, and such corrections correlated with that of the corrections made in Septuagint by the original scribes from fourth century to the twelfth century. Corrections were made not with an idea to insert new ideas but to make the text better readable, understandable and to give better insights as the text was copied from one generation to the next by the successive scribes.

---

[35] Greek: Σιναϊτικός Κώδικας, Hebrew: קודק סינאיטיקו; Shelfmarks and references: London, Brit. Libr., Additional Manuscripts 43725; Gregory-Aland nº ℵ [Aleph] or 01, [Soden δ 2]) or "Sinai Bible" is one of the four great uncial codices, an ancient, handwritten copy of the Greek Bible. (Credits to Wikipedia)

[36] Metzger, Bruce; Bart D. Ehrman (2005). The Text of the New Testament: An Introduction to the Critical Editions and to the Theory and Practice of Modern Textual Criticism. New York – Oxford: Oxford University Press. p. 62. ISBN 978-0-19-516122-9.

How the Bible Came To Us

This Codex had the Old Testament and the New Testament in full along with few of the apocrypha books, namely, 1 Esdras, 2 Esdras, Tobit, Judith, and 1 and 4 Maccabees, Wisdom and Sirach. It also had "Epistle of Barnabas" and "The Shepherd" of Hermas, as appendix to the New Testament. Those additional books were later banned from the Protestant Bible.

It appalls us to know the discovery of the codex Sinaiticus and the way God preserved His Word. It was found along with lot of wastepaper ready to be burnt to bring warmth to the St. Catherine's monastery at the foot of Mount Sainai, when the weather was too cold. It is no surprise that monasteries get cold and they need material to burn and keep them warm. They did not realize the importance of codex Sinaiticus and put them as trash for burning. However, God did not lose sight of their negligence and sent someone of His choice to collect it.

A Biblical scholar, whose name was Constantin Tischendorf, an excellent Bible scholar, found this codex in the waste bin, and realizing its importance he quickly picked it up. Tischendorf was born in a town called "Lengenfeld" near Plauen, Saxony (a free state in Germany), to a physician, and spent his scholarly education at the University of Leipzig. This scholar discovered the first part of Codex Sinaiticus in 1844 and its second part in 1859.

The arrangement of the books in the Bible gained importance from this codex where it was found that the letter to the Hebrews was place after II Epistle of Paul to the Thessalonians, although in canonical Bible it took a different order. The construction of the Christian Bible had its roots in Codex Sinaiticus, which surpassed Codex Vaticanus in importance.

How the Bible Came To Us

Codex Sinaiticus was of high technical improvement in manufacturing and binding seven hundred and thirty large leaflets into book format.

BIBLIOGRAPHY

Tischendorf, 1862. Constantin Tischendorf, *Bibliorum Codex Sinaiticus Petropolitanus*. St. Petersburg, 1862. 4 vols
Lake, Helen, and Kirsopp Lake. Codex Sinaiticus Petropolitanus. 2 vols. Oxford: Clarendon, 1911-1922.

How the Bible Came To Us

CODEX SINAITICUS

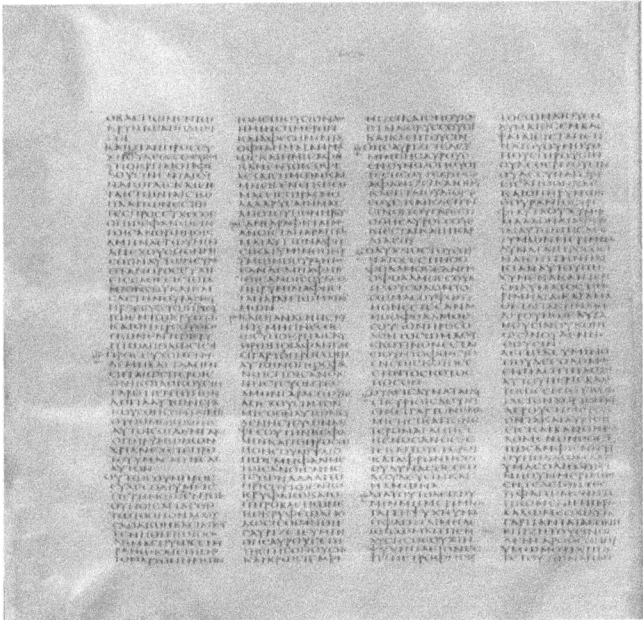

"codex sinaiticus" Public Domain {{PD-1923}} Description English: page of the codex with text of Matthew 6:4-32. Date 4th century. Source Codex Sinaiticus. Author Unknown.
http://www.codexsinaiticus.org/en/manuscript.aspx?book=33&chapter=6&lid=en&side=r&verse=12&zoomSlider=0

There were also lesser important codices namely...

1. CODEX EPHRAEMI[37]
2. CODEX LAUDIANUS[38]
3. CODEX REGIUS[39]

---

[37] Paris, National Library of France, Greek 9; Gregory-Aland no. C or 04, von Soden δ)
[38] designated by Ea or 08 (in the Gregory-Aland numbering), α 1001 (von Soden)
[39] Latin: Cōdex Rēgius, "(The) Royal Book"; Icelandic: Konungsbók) or GKS

CHAPTER 18
CODEX VATICANUS

Text according to Comfort
Recto
α
[1:1] βιβλος γενεσεως ΙΥ ΧΥ ΥΥ δαυιδ [ΥΥ]
αβρααμ [1:2] αβρααμ εγεννησεν τον [ισαακ]
ισαακ δ[ε] εγεννησεν τ[ον] ιακωβ [ιακωβ]
δε εγ[ε]ννησεν τον ιουδαν κ[α]ι τ[ους]
α[δ]ελφους αυτου [1:3] ιουδας δε εγεννη
σεν τον φαρες και τον ζαρε εκ της θα
μαρ φαρες δε εγεννησεν τον εσρωμ
εσ[ρω]μ δε εγεννησεν τ[ο]ν αραμ [1:4] α[ραμ]
δε [ε]γεννησεν τον αμμιναδαβ αμ
μ[ι]ναδ[α]β δε εγεννησεν τον ναασσων
ναα[σ]σων δε εγενν[ησ]εν τον σαλ[μω]ν
[1:5] σαλμων δε εγενν[η]σεν τον βοες [εκ]
της ραχαβ βοες δε εγεννησεν τον ι
ωβηδ εκ της ρ[ο]υθ ιω[βηδ δ]ε εγεννη
σεν τον ιεσσαι [1:6] ιεσσ[αι] δε εγεννησεν
τον δαυιδ τον βασιλε[α δαυ]ιδ δε εγεν
νησεν τον σολομωνα εκ της ουρειου. [1:7] σο
λομων δε εγεννησεν τον [ρ]οβοαμ ροβο
αμ δε εγεννησεν τ[ο]ν [αβει]α αβεια δε
εγεννησεν [το]ν ασα[φ] [1:8] [α]σ[α]φ δε εγεν

2365 4to is an Icelandic codex

How the Bible Came To Us

νησεν τον ιωσαφατ ι[ω]σαφατ δ[ε] εγεν

ν[η]σε[ν] τον ιωραμ ιωραμ δε εγεν[νησεν

τον] οζε[ι]αν [1:9] οζειας δε εγεν[νησεν]
lacuna [1:12] lacuna [με
τοικεσιαν βαβυλωνος ιεχονι]ας εγ[εν
νησεν] lacuna

[40]Copyright information

Verso
[1:14] [lacuna] β
[τον σ]αδω[κ σ]αδωκ δε εγεννησεν το[ν
αχειμ] αχειμ δε εγε[ν]νησεν τον ελιου[δ]
[1:15] [ελιου]δ δε εγ[εν]νη[σ]ε[ν] τον ελεαζαρ ελε
[αζ]αρ [δε εγ]εννησεν [το]ν μαθθαν μαθθα[ν]
δε εγεννη[σ]εν τον [ι]ακωβ [1:16] ιακωβ δε
[εγ]εννησεν τον ιωσηφ τον ανδρα μ[α]
ριας [ε]ξ ης εγενν[ηθ]η ΙΣ ο λεγομενο[ς ΧΣ]
[1:17] πασαι ουν γε[νε]αι απο αβρααμ εως
δαυιδ γενεαι ΙΔ και απο [δ]α[υ]ιδ [ε]ως τη[ς]
μετοικεσιας βαβυλωνο[ς] γε[νεαι] ΙΔ κα[ι]
απο της μετ[οι]κεσιας βαβ[υ]λων[ο]ς εως
του ΧΥ γενεαι [Ι]Δ [1:18] του δε ΙΥ ΧΥ η γενε
σις ουτως ην μνηστε[υ]θεισης της μη
τρος αυτου μ[αρι]α[ς] τω [ιω]σηφ πριν η συν
[ε]λθε[ι]ν αυ[το]υ[ς] ευρε[θη] εν γαστρι εχου

---

[40] http://creativecommons.org/licenses/by-sa/3.0/deed.en_US {{PD-US}}

σα ε[κ ΠΝΣ αγιου] [1:19] [ιωσηφ δε ο] ανηρ αυ
της [δι]και[ος ων και μη θελων αυτην]
δειγμα[τ]ε[ισαι εβουλη]θη [λαθρα
α]πολυ[σαι] α[υ]τ[η]ν [1:20] [τ]αυτα [δε αυτου εν
θ]υμη[θεντος ι]δου αγ[γελο]ς ΚΥ [κ]α[τ
ο]ναρ [εφανη αυ]τω [λεγων] ιωσ[η]φ
υιος] δ[αυιδ] μ[η] φο[βηθη]ς παρ[αλαβ]ει
[μ]αριαν [την] γυναι[κα σου] το [γαρ εν αυ
τη γεν]νηθεν ε[κ] ΠΝΣ [εστιν] α[γιου]
[1:21-23] lacuna
με[θερμηνευομενον μεθ ημων ο ΘΣ]

Disagreement with Vaticanus (according to Hoskier[41])

Papyrus 1	Vaticanus
ΥΥ	ΥΙΟΥ
ΔΑΥΙΔ	ΔΑΥΕΙΔ
ΑΜΙΝΑΔΑΒ	
ΔΑΥΙΔ	ΑΜΕΙΝΑΔΑΒ
ΤΗΣ ΟΥΡΕΙΟΥ	ΔΑΥΕΙΔ
ΑΒ[ΕΙ]Α	ΤΗΣ ΤΟΥ ΟΥΡΕΙΟΥ
ΑΒΕΙΑ	ΑΒΙΑ
ΕΓΕ[ΝΗΣΕΝ]	ΑΒΙΑ
illeg	ΓΕΝΝΑ
illeg	ΤΟΝ ΣΕΛΑΘΙΗΛ
illeg	ΣΕΛΑΘΙΗΛ ΔΕ ΓΕΝΝΑ
ΜΑΘΘΑΝ	ΑΒΙΟΥΤ
ΙΩΣΗΦ	ΜΑΤΘΑΝ
ΓΕΝΕΑΙ	ΤΟΝ ΙΩΣΗΦ
ΔΑΥΙΔ	ΑΙ ΓΕΝΕΑΙ
ΔΑΥΙΔ	ΔΑΥΕΙΔ

---

[41] Hoskier, Codex B and Its Allies, a study and an indictment, Bernard Quaritch (London 1914), p. XI

How the Bible Came To Us

ΙΔ	ΔΑΥΕΙΔ
ΙΥ ΧΥ	ΔΕΚΑΤΕΣΣΑΡΕΣ
ΔΕΙΓΜΑ[Τ]ΕΙΣΑΙ	ΧΥ ΙΥ
ΔΑΥΙΔ	ΔΕΙΓΜΑΤΙΣΑΙ
	ΔΑΥΕΙΔ[6]

---

[42]Copyright information

---

[42] http://creativecommons.org/licenses/by-sa/3.0/deed.en_US {{PD-US}}

[43]Copyright information and [44]Bibliography

---

[43] http://creativecommons.org/licenses/by-sa/3.0/deed.en_US
[43] http://ntvmr.uni-muenster.de/manuscript-workspace/?docID=10001

[44] Epp, Eldon J. "The New Testament Papyri at Oxyrhynchus in Their Social and Intellectual Context." In *Sayings of Jesus: Canonical and Non-Canonical: Essays in Honour of Tjitze Baarda,* edited by William L. Petersen, 46–68. Leiden [u.a.], 1997.
Head, Peter M. "Observations on Early Papyri of the Synoptic Gospels, Especially on the 'Scribal Habits.'" *Biblica: Commentarii Periodici Pontificii Institutii Biblici* 71 (1990): 240–47.
INTF. "Hänger 10001," 2014.
O'Callaghan, José. "Mt 2,14 En El Fragmento Adéspota de P1?" *Studia Papyrologica: Revista Espanola de Papirologia* 10, no. 2 (1971): 87–92.
Sanders, Henry A. "The Egyptian Text of the Four Gospels and Acts." *The Harvard Theological Review* 26, no. 2 (1933): 77–98.
Soden, Hermann von. *Die Schriften Des Neuen Testaments. Teil 1: Untersuchungen. Abt. 2: Die Textformen: A. Die Evangelien.* 2 (unverändert). Vol. 1,2. 2 vols. Göttingen: Vandenhoeck u. Ruprecht, 1911

How the Bible Came To Us

PAGE FROM ALEPPO CODEX DEUTERONOMY[45]

Source: Public Domain

---

[45] A page from Deuteronomy. Aleppo Codex, n.d. web[29 May 2015] <http://www.aleppocodex.org/links/8.html>

CHAPTER 19
APOCRYPHA BOOKS

The Protestant Bible, as we have today, is a collection of sixty six books with thirty nine in the Old Testament and twenty seven in the New Testament. There were many manuscripts and books and writings available from the time of Moses until apostolic period in the New Testament era, but not all of them were included in the Bible. Out of several books and writings available only sixty six books were chosen to be in the Bible. There is a good reason not to include all of them in the Bible.

Apocrypha[46],[47],[48] means:

"A group of 14 books, not considered canonical, included in the Septuagint and the Vulgate as part of the Old Testament, but usually omitted from Protestant editions of the Bible[49]". These texts were included in Septuagint but not in the Hebrew Bible and they are of unknown authorship or spurious in the context of Bibles of Jews and Christians. However, Martin Luther said "Apocrypha — that is, books which are not regarded as equal to the Holy Scriptures, and yet are profitable and good to read.[50]"

"In the beginning was the Word, and the Word was with God, and the Word was God" (John 1:1)

---

[46] The Bible: Authorized King James Version with Apocrypha, Oxford World's Classics, 2008 Print
[47] Josephus, Against Apion 1. 8
[48] Wikipedia
[49] Dictionary n.d. Web [05 May, 2015] <http://www.dictionary.com>
[50] King James Version Defended page 98

How the Bible Came To Us

No man has written the Word of God as he intended it to be, or compiled it as he intended it to be. The Word was already there in the beginning, and the Word was with God, and the Word was God. Psalmist writes:

"Forever, O LORD, your word is settled in heaven" Psalm 119:89

"The words of the LORD *are* pure words: *as* silver tried in a furnace of earth, purified seven times" Psalm 12:6

Inspired men wrote the Inspired Scriptures and only the books of the Bible that were recognized as genuine, and inspired by the Christian Church found way into the canonized Bible. A set of books chosen to be in the Bible by an ecclesiastical rule or law enacted by a council by the early Church were made to be part of one great book called "Bible".

The Apocryphal books of King James Version are:

1. 1 Esdras
2. 2 Esdras
3. Tobit
4. Judith
5. Rest of Esther
6. Wisdom
7. Ecclesiasticus
8. Baruch and the Epistle of Jeremy
9. Song of the Three Children
10. Story of Susanna
11. The Idol Bel and the Dragon
12. Prayer of Manasses
13. 1 Maccabees
14. 2 Maccabees

How the Bible Came To Us

Apocryphal books were neither of the same standard as of Hebrew Scriptures, nor did they seemed to be inspired Word of God; rather there was consensus among Hebrew scholars to categorize them as spurious documents, written either to propagate pet theories of theologians, or to please the Jews who were either under captivity or were not facing amiable situations.

In Addition, Jewish Historian Flavius Josephus identified [in Contra Apion 1:7-8] twenty two books as belonging to Hebrew Scripture, which was equivalent to 39 of the Protestant Old Testament.

A contemporary Biblical Scholar named Jerome (325- 420 A.D), who translated the Catholic Bible into "vulgate", which is Latin version of the Bible used by the Roman Catholic Church, did not include apocryphal books in the Latin vulgate. Jewish historian's mentioning of number of books in the Hebrew Scripture matched with Jerome's Latin vulgate, which had only thirty nine books same as of Protestant Bible.

It was this reason that the theologians and scholars, who debated over canonization of the Bible, had tough time dealing with the controversy, as to the number of books and the names of the books to be included in the Bible. The debate could be traced back until Hebrew Scriptures were translated into Greek, and such translation of Hebrew Scriptures into Greek Scriptures was called "Septuagint".

How the Bible Came To Us

CHAPTER 20
INERRANCY AND INFALLIBILTY

INERRANCY

Inerrancy according to dictionary has two meanings.

1. lack of error; infallibility
2. The belief that the Bible is free from error in matters of science as well as those of faith.

The Holy Bible has no errors as far as doctrinal position is concerned. That is to say the Bible contains neither material errors nor internal contradictions and no errors of faith.

Many misunderstand the term "inerrancy" and immaturely conclude that Bible has errors. If inerrancy is to be understood as perfectness, without any errors, then it should be attributed only to the originals, which were called 'autographs'.

There are errors, of course, in matters of spelling and grammar etc., because the originals perished over time, due to inclement weather affecting the parchments and papyrus scrolls on which scriptures were handwritten, and kept under different conditions on different terrains. With all the modern facilities available for us, our Bibles suffer wear and tear in one lifetime or two generations, unless preserved very carefully. It is then, no wonder the feeble and frail material upon which the script was handwritten perished over many centuries.

Fragments of papyrus, and parchments that were found had been carefully collected, and the best of scholars compiled them into codex (book-form). There was no scope of fraudulently compiling them as they desired because the

How the Bible Came To Us

number of great scholars who compiled them were many in number. They meticulously codified each section, counted the number of verses, words and letters in the text. The Tanakh, as the Jews call their Hebrew Bible as, it is the "Old Testament" for Christians.

Genesis 11:1 reads...

"And the whole earth was of one language and of one speech"

This language was Hebrew language which Moses spoke and wrote. As men thought of establishing human government, and ventured to build a tall tower at Babel, with in intention of reaching heaven by their own efforts, God destroyed their plans and confused their languages.

Not once, but several times men disobeyed God and incurred His wrath. Therefore, although God gave His inspired Word to men, yet He did not supervise transmission of His word from generation to generation, as the languages and dialects changed. This was the cause for imperfect transmission of the Word of God.

HEBREW LANGUAGE

Hebrew Language is distinct and unique inasmuch as it is semantic and not just phonetic, whereas all other languages on the planet earth depend on phonetics for pronouncing the words and understanding their meaning. Surprisingly in the case of Hebrew language if one knows the meaning of the letter one can know what the combination of the letters would mean.

Moreover, Hebrew language had no vowels, and no space between words, and yet the language was self-parsing. There are five letters that are slightly different in shape, and if anyone

How the Bible Came To Us

of them is the last letter in the word, one can read the sentence even if there was no space between the words.

Hebrew is God's language, and it was, and it is still the pride language of Israel. It was that marvelous language, which had almost become extinct after 70 AD, when Jerusalem was destroyed by Titus, and during the diaspora of Israel, but it resuscitated after 1948, when Israel became an independent Nation.

A great deal of time passed before printing press was invented. Godly men in their best have translated the Bible into different languages and passed the scriptures from generation to generation. Obviously, human element was involved and, therefore, minor errors have crept into the scripture and yet the central doctrines of the Bible never changed in any generation; and this is how "inerrancy" should be understood.

INFALLIBILITY

"All scripture is given by inspiration of God, and is profitable for doctrine, for reproof, for correction, for instruction in righteousness: That the man of God may be perfect, throughly furnished unto all good works"   2 Timothy 3:16, 17

The Scriptures are subjective consequence of divine inspiration. They are reliable and trustworthy to all who obey them diligently and search the knowledge of the Truth. To those who deliberately oppose the Scriptures, they do not make any sense, as God's Word says that the preaching of the message of cross is foolishness to them that perish, but unto them who are saved, it is the power of God. Paul preached the Gospel of Jesus Christ but it was foolishness to Greeks.

How the Bible Came To Us

"For the preaching of the cross is to them that perish foolishness; but unto us which are saved it is the power of God" (1 Corinthians 1:18)

How the Bible Came To Us

CHAPTER 21
THE TRANSMISSION

Papyrus was fragile and frail material on which the scribes imprinted the scriptures. However, over time the papyri were getting destroyed and the script was getting lost. In order to preserve the text on these papyri scholars copied the scriptures to new papyri and thus the old ones perished.

The original documents are called "autographs" and those original documents are no more there. What the scholars discovered were only fragments of papyri and copies. The copies were copied and thus copies of copies were made available. After the printing press was invented there were more errors in the scripts and thus in the first KJV it is said that there were four hundred errors.

Nevertheless, all these errors were related to copying errors, such as spelling mistakes, and grammatical errors; otherwise the central doctrine of the relationship of the Father and the Son, and of the Holy Spirit were never compromised, either in the Roman Catholic Church or Protestant Church. There was, no doubt, misinterpretation of scriptures by various denominations.

"Study to shew thyself approved unto God, a workman that needeth not to be ashamed, rightly dividing the word of truth" (2 Timothy 2:15)

If we go through the Scriptures in their context supported by other related scriptures convincing interpretations will evolve. This is what "rightly dividing the word of truth" means. All scriptures are given for correction, reproof and admonition.

How the Bible Came To Us

"All scripture is given by inspiration of God, and is profitable for doctrine, for reproof, for correction, for instruction in righteousness: That the man of God may be perfect, throughly furnished unto all good works" (2 Timothy 3:16-17)

IMPERFECT TRANSMISSION

A great deal of work was involved in transmission of the Word of God, by copying and copying the copied texts, translating the texts. The imperfectness in transmission between the writer and the reader was influenced by cultural, historical, rhetorical gaps. Yet, in all these adverse situations, the Scriptures that are considered as disputed ones measure only up to 1%.

It is so comforting to note that none of those disputed passages are the reasons for interpreting or misinterpreting soteriology (the doctrine of salvation through Jesus Christ).

How the Bible Came To Us

CHAPTER 22
DEAD SEA SCROLLS

It was a fascinating discovery in 1947 AD, of about 980 scrolls, in the caves known as "Qumran" on the banks of the Dead Sea that lead to give more credence to the writings of the Bible. It was a casual walk into the cave by a Bedouin boy shepherding his flock when one of his goats lost its way. The boy went in search of the goat and threw a stone into the cave surmising that the goat would be there. Instead, the stone hit a jar and the boy heard a shattering noise. The boy was curious about the noise and entered into the cave and was disappointed for finding a jar and many scrolls wrapped in linen. The boy took all of them and hung at his tent and later sold to inquisitive Jew for a paltry sum worth $4.00.

To the Jew the scrolls he bought were like a great treasure as expounded them. They were written in Hebrew, Aramaic and Greek languages. The Jew's help led researchers and scholars to delve into more research and to find the secrecy of the scrolls. Their research fetched them many more scrolls and as the time went by the engineers developed them into digital formats and placed them in the museum at Jerusalem.

The scrolls written in three different languages are of great significance, both in religious and historical aspects. They were significant, to those who followed Judaism and Christianity, because they included the oldest surviving manuscripts that were included later when the Old Testament was canonized.

Apart from Biblical texts that were in Hebrew, Greek, and Aramaic, other texts that were found were in Latin and in

How the Bible Came To Us

different dialects as well. While some texts were written on Papyrus most of them were on parchments.

Jewish historian Flavius Josephus mentions in his book of a sect called "Essenes"[51] who, perhaps, in rebellion against the ruling priests at Jerusalem, left their abode and went and lived in the Judean plains, which were at the lowest elevation on the earth. They believed that they were the right inheritors of the kingdom of God, because they lived more pious life, and waited for the end of the world. Perhaps, in their dejection, of not seeing the end of the evil world, many committed suicide, and the descendants of the rest are unrecognizable now.

It is believed that these sects wrote and preserved the invaluable texts for future generations to explore. It is true that the scrolls found in the eleven caves at Qumran site were the result of such preservation. Those scrolls corroborated with the original texts found on fragments that later became the Hebrew Bible.

Large amount of texts found belonged to the texts of the Hebrew Bible, while some belonged to the period when Zerubbabel Temple was standing, and some belonged to sectarian groups defining their rules, regulations etc. All those texts that belonged to Zerubbabel Temple period and not appeared in the original Hebrew texts on parchments and papyrus were rejected to be included in the canonical Bible; and such rejected texts include Apocrypha books, namely, 1 Esdras, 2 Esdras, Tobit , Judith, Wisdom of Solomon, Ecclesiasticus,

---

[51] Flavius Josephus. The Jewish War, Book II, Chapter 8:2:119

How the Bible Came To Us

Baruch, Letter of Jeremiah, Prayer of Azariah, Susanna, Bel and the Dragon, Prayer of Manasseh, 1 Maccabees, 2 Maccabees.

Apocryphal books that were rejected to be included in the canonical Bible were "Book of Jubilees", "Book of Enoch", "Gospel of Thomas", "Apocalypse of Peter" etc.

The Dead Sea Scrolls[52] caught the attention of researchers from American Schools of Oriental Research (ASOR). They carefully compared the scripts on the scrolls with that of the oldest manuscripts of Tanakh and found great similarities between them. As the monetary value of the excavated increased the Bedouins and the ASOR researchers increased their pace of research in the caves of Qumran and surrounding areas, where in 1956 final fragments were found.

The Great Isaiah Scroll[53]

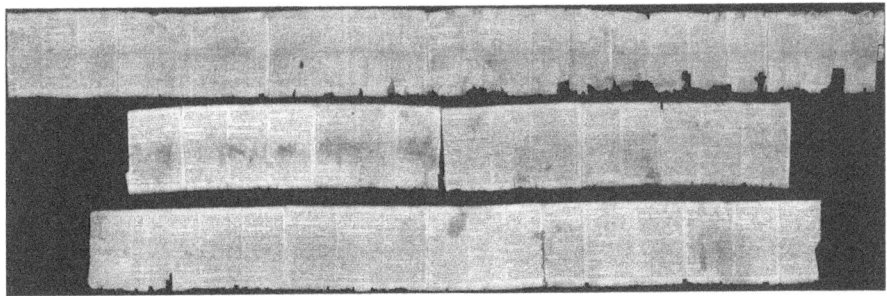

(In Public Domain)

---

[52] "Dead Sea Scrolls" Wikipedia n.d.Web[22 May, 2015
[53] "Great Isaiah Scroll" by Photographs by Ardon Bar Hama, author of original document is unknown. - Website of The Israel Museum, Jerusalem, see link.. Licensed under Public Domain via Wikimedia Commons - http://commons.wikimedia.org/wiki/File:Great_Isaiah_Scroll.jpg#/media/File:Great_Isaiah_Scroll.jpg

How the Bible Came To Us

CHAPTER 23
THE GIST OF APOCRYPHA BOOKS

APOCRYPHA BOOKS [54]

APOCRYPHA is different from APOCRYPHAL. Apocrypha Books are specific number of Books placed after Old Testament and before New Testament. In some editions there are fifteen apocrypha books and in some fourteen. None of these books were available in Hebrew Bible, nor are accepted by Protestant Christians as inspired Scriptures, and therefore, they are not in our present Holy Bible. Until 1885 A.D the apocrypha books were in the King James Bible 1611 edition. However, after 274 years of their existence as part of King James Bible they were removed from the Bible. Their position in the Bible was after the Old Testament and before the New Testament. They were also known as "deuterocanonical books" by the Catholic Church.

Septuagint included them only for the historical reasons and in the Latin Vulgate they are placed at the end of Old Testament. King James Bible 1611 has the Apocrypha at the end of the Old Testament; however, in the latest editions apocrypha is removed.

The fundamental reason for their removal from the Bible is that they are not considered as inspired scriptures; they are considered as spurious writings with no doctrinal teachings; historian Flavius Joseph recognized only 22 books which is equivalent to present 39 books in the Old Testament; New Testament readings do not quote any passages from apocrypha;

---

[54] - King James Bible "Authorized Version", Cambridge Edition

How the Bible Came To Us

and Lord Jesus Christ referred prophets as from Abel unto Zechariah in II Chronicles 24:20-21; Matthew 23:35.

An excerpt from the preface of the first ever full-length Geneva English Bible without apocrypha published in 1560 A.D. reads as follows:

Quote[55]: *The books that follow in order after the Prophets unto the New Testament, are called Apocrypha, that is, books which were not received by a common consent to be read and expounded publicly in the Church, neither yet served to prove any point of Christian religion save in so much as they had the consent of the other scriptures called canonical to confirm the same, or rather whereon they were grounded: but as books proceeding from godly men they were received to be read for the advancement and furtherance of the knowledge of history and for the instruction of godly manners: which books declare that at all times God had an especial care of His Church, and left them not utterly destitute of teachers and means to confirm them in the hope of the promised Messiah, and also witness that those calamities that God sent to his Church were according to his providence, who had both so threatened by his prophets, and so brought it to pass, for the destruction of their enemies and for the trial of his children.* Unquote

The following are the Apocrypha books included in the King James Bible 1611 version[56]

1. 1 Esdras
2. 2 Esdras

---

[55] Benham, William. "The Dictionary of Religion". Cassel & Company, Ltd. New York 1887 Print. (PP 55-56)

[56] "The Official King James Bible online" 1611 King James Bible, n.d. Web [08 May, 2015]

3. Tobit
4. Judith
5. Additions to Esther
6. Wisdom of Solomon
7. Ecclesiasticus
8. Baruch
9. Letter of Jeremiah
10. Prayer of Azariah
11. Susanna
12. Bel and the Dragon
13. Prayer of Manasseh
14. 1 Maccabees
15. 2 Maccabees

Apocryphal books are forgery books namely Gospel of Thomas, etc. The content of these books are Gnostic and purely heretic. Apocryphal stories are false and spurious.

1 ESDRAS [57]

Some unknown author attempted to add text of the last two chapters of 2 Chronicles and the last two chapters of Nehemiah to the Book of Ezra along with a fictitious story. The story was about three young courtiers debating as to what is the strongest thing or strongest one in the world. The first courtier argues that it is the vine; the second one argues that it is the king, and the third argues that God is the strongest one. The Persian King before whom the debate was held awards to Zerubbabel, who was the third courtier, much lured prize of rebuilding Jerusalem.

---

[57] "1 Esdras", Apocrypha. KJV Bible, 1611 Ed. n.d. Web[05 May, 2015]

How the Bible Came To Us

2 ESDRAS [58]

An unknown author edited the Jewish revelations of the ultimate divine purpose, which seemed to have been written, as some say in Greek, and as some say in Hebrew and translated into Latin. The book is missing its roots in Septuagint manuscripts, and therefore, Greek text is not available to anyone. The contents of the book largely deal with dialogue between Ezra the scribe and the angels about the evil and afflictions of Israel. It corroborates the view that this book is a fictitious work written to encourage Jews who suffered destruction in AD 70 at the hands of Titus. A fantastic story that three-headed eagle, symbolic of Roman Empire, which would finally be destroyed by a roaring lion, symbolic of Messiah, found its way into this book. Martin Luther omitted the two books of Esdras from his German Bible and so did the Roman Catholic Church at the council of Trent in 1516.

TOBIT [59]

It contains, supposedly, a fictitious story of a Jewish family that was forcibly moved to Nineveh during Babylonian captivity of Jews. A blind man by name Tobit sends his son Tobias on a task of collecting a debt. An angel (probably Raphael) appears to him on his way and invites to a house, where a virgin whose seven husbands were killed one after another by a demon, before anyone of them had consummation with her. Tobias, who was a compassionate man, marries the virgin and drives the demon away from her house by burning in her bedroom the heart of a peculiar fish with the help of Raphael. He returns to his home not only with the collected debt, but also with the virgin, whom

---

[58] "2 Esdras", Apocrypha. KJV Bible, 1611 Ed. n.d. Web[05 May, 2015]
[59] "Tobit", Apocrypha. KJV Bible 1611 Ed. n.d. Web[07 May, 2015]

How the Bible Came To Us

he married. The gall of the fish, which he burnt, is used by him to heal his father's eyes. After the natural death of his father Tobit, he leaves the city of Nineveh, which is judged and destroyed. The story was originally written in Aramaic and subsequently translated into Greek. Obviously, the text did not find a place in the Inspired Scriptures.

Tobit teaches that salvation can be obtained by doing good works, a doctrine which is not accepted by Protestant Christians.

"For almsgiving saves from death and purges away every sin. Those who give alms will enjoy a full life" (Tobit 12:9).

New Testament teaches that salvation is by grace through faith.

"For by grace you are saved through faith, and this is not your own doing; it is the gift of God - not the result of works, so that no one may boast" (Ephesians 2:8,9).

JUDITH [60]

Unlike Esther, who in the book of Esther, one of the thirty nine books approved as inspired scripture, Judith in one of the apocryphal books has a vile strategy in helping Jews. The two characters depicted in the two books are quite contrary to each other. The book of Judith was supposedly written circa 150 B.C. in Hebrew, and translated into Greek; however the Greek Text is no more available. Judith, a widow successfully sneaks into enemy camp and entices the general that she would give vital secret information about Jews to him and secures confidence in her. The enemy general believes her and gets drunk along with

---

[60] "Judith", KJV Bible. 1611 Ed, n.d. Web[07 May 2015]
  Wikipedia

her when Judith slays him. She then brings the general's head into the camp of Jews whose faith is increased by seeing her courage and the snapped head of the enemy General. The Assyrians are morally discouraged on losing their General and flee leaving behind the city of Jews and thus Israel is saved. The text is so unbelievable inasmuch as she does not marry anyone but concedes herself to be courted although she was keen on keeping the Law of Moses. A glaring example of historical error[61] is in Judith 1:1

"It was the twelfth year of the reign of Nebuchadnezzar, who ruled over the Assyrians in the great city of Nineveh. In those days Arphaxad ruled over the Medes in Ecbatana" (Judith 1:1).

ADDITIONS TO ESTHER [62]

St. Jerome sorted out six long paragraphs occurring in several places from Septuagint version of the Esther and put them at the end of the Book of Esther while translating the Bible into 'vulgate'. The hidden hand of God helping Jews was very much there although God's name is not mentioned in the Book of Esther. However, from the text interspersed in six different locations deliberately brings in the name of God. Jerome accepted the additions to Esther as canonical, but thought they were inserted by unknown Jew from Egypt. These verses seemed to sympathetically speak in favor of Jews that they were delivered from their Gentile enemies who devised evil against them.

---

[61] Stewart, Don. "Don Stewart :: What Are the Contents of the Various Books of the Old Testament Apocrypha?." Blue Letter Bible. Sowing Circle. 24 Apr, 2007. Web. 8 May, 2015.
<http://www.blueletterbible.org/faq/don_stewart/don_stewart_392.cfm>.
[62] "Additions to Esther". Apocrypha. KJV Bible, 1611 Ed. n.d. Web[05 May, 2015]

How the Bible Came To Us

WISDOM OF SOLOMON [63]

An unknown Jew from Alexandria wrote few devotional essays in Greek purportedly as discourses from King Solomon. This book is also known as "Wisdom" and it teaches pre-existence of souls.

"For I was a witty child, and had a good spirit. Yea rather being good, I came into a body undefiled" Wisdom 8:19, 20

"So now, my children see what almsgiving accomplishes, and what injustice does it brings death!" (Tobit 14:11).

Christian writers appreciate the writings, but they do not seem to be original writings. There was comparison of Greek philosophy with Judaism and it proposes that faith is the highest form of wisdom.

ECCLESIASTICUS [64]

This book is a quite big with fifty one chapters and not to be confused with Old Testametn Canonical Book Ecclesiastes. It was originally called "Sirach" or "The wisdom of Jesus son of Sirach". Author Joshua Ben Sirach wrote this book in Hebrew, which was translated into Greek by his grandson. The text does not contain inspired text but contains common life discourses about religious faith and life. As Martin Luther said, this book is good for reading, but not worth including in the Bible. The proverbs and sayings in this book had good quality poetry.

---

[63] Stewart, Don. "Don Stewart :: Why Were the Books of the Old Testament Apocrypha Rejected as Holy Scripture by the Protestants?." Blue Letter Bible. Sowing Circle. 24 Apr, 2007. Web. 8 May, 2015.
<http://www.blueletterbible.org/faq/don_stewart/don_stewart_395.cfm>.
[64] "THE OFFICIAL KINGS JAMES BIBLE ONLINE" Ecclesiasticus, n.d. Web[08 May, 2015]

How the Bible Came To Us

Some Interesting verses from Ecclesiasticus Chapter 49 [65]

"12 So was Jesus the son of Josedec: who in their time builded the house, and set up an holy temple to the Lord, which was prepared for everlasting glory. 13 And among the elect was Neemias, whose renown is great, who raised up for us the walls that were fallen, and set up the gates and the bars, and raised up our ruins again. 14 But upon the earth was no man created like Enoch; for he was taken from the earth. 15 Neither was there a young man born like Joseph, a governor of his brethren, a stay of the people, whose bones were regarded of the Lord. 16 Sem and Seth were in great honour among men, and so was Adam above every living thing in creation".

BARUCH [66]

This book could not have been written before 150 B.C, and yet it is projected as if it was written by Baruch, a disciple of Jeremiah when the children of Israel were under Babylonian captivity. The contents of the book are, no doubt, appealing that God is against idolatry, keeping the Law of Moses, encouragement, promises etc. and yet because they were not the scriptures in the Jewish Bible (Tanakh) the book Baruch is removed from the Bible when it was canonized.

The first ten verses from Baruch Chapter 1 read as follows:

Quote: 1 And these are the words of the book, which Baruch the son of Nerias, the son of Maasias, the son of Sedecias, the son of Asadias, the son of Chelcias, wrote in Babylon, 2 In the fifth year, and in the seventh day of the month, what time as the

---

[65] [- *King James Bible "Authorized Version", Cambridge Edition*]

[66] [- *King James Bible "Authorized Version", Cambridge Edition*]

How the Bible Came To Us

Chaldeans took Jerusalem, and burnt it with fire. 3 And Baruch did read the words of this book in the hearing of Jechonias the son of Joachim king of Juda, and in the ears of all the people that came to hear the book, 4 And in the hearing of the nobles, and of the king's sons, and in the hearing of the elders, and of all the people, from the lowest unto the highest, even of all them that dwelt at Babylon by the river Sud. 5 Whereupon they wept, fasted, and prayed before the Lord. 6 They made also a collection of money according to every man's power: 7 And they sent it to Jerusalem unto Joachim the high priest, the son of Chelcias, son of Salom, and to the priests, and to all the people which were found with him at Jerusalem, 8 At the same time when he received the vessels of the house of the Lord, that were carried out of the temple, to return them into the land of Juda, the tenth day of the month Sivan, namely, silver vessels, which Sedecias the son of Josias king of Jada had made, 9 After that Nabuchodonosor king of Babylon had carried away Jechonias, and the princes, and the captives, and the mighty men, and the people of the land, from Jerusalem, and brought them unto Babylon. 10 And they said, Behold, we have sent you money to buy you burnt offerings, and sin offerings, and incense, and prepare ye manna, and offer upon the altar of the Lord our God; Unquote

- Baruch was not really in Babylon 1:1,2 compare Jer.43:5-7
- Baruch says the Jews would serve Babylon for 7 generations as against Jeremiah 25:11 which says they serve Babylon for 70 years;

But Johanan the son of Kareah, and all the captains of the forces, took all the remnant of Judah, that were returned from all nations, whither they had been driven, to dwell in the land of

How the Bible Came To Us

Judah; Even men, and women, and children, and the king's daughters, and every person that Nebuzaradan the captain of the guard had left with Gedaliah the son of Ahikam the son of Shaphan, and Jeremiah the prophet, and Baruch the son of Neriah. So they came into the land of Egypt: for they obeyed not the voice of the LORD: thus came they even to Tahpanhes. (Jeremiah 43:5-7)

Catholic Bible has 6 chapters in Baruch as against King James Bible 1611 has only 5 chapters in Baruch. The sixth Chapter of Catholic Bible is obviously another apocrypha Book called "Epistle of Jeremiah". Catholic Bible Baruch 6:2 ("Epistle of Jeremiah")reads:

"Once you have reached Babylon you will stay there for many years, as long as seven generations; after which I shall bring you home in peace". Baruch 6:2

"And this whole land shall be a desolation, and an astonishment; and these nations shall serve the king of Babylon seventy years" (Jeremiah 25:11)

LETTER OF JEREMIAH [67]

Whereas this book is shown as 6th Chapter in the Apocrypha book of "Baruch" in the Catholic Bible, it occupies as an independent book in KJB 1611 English Bible.

"2. Because of the sins which ye have committed before God, ye shall be led away captives into Babylon by Nabuchodonosor king of the Babylonians. 3. So when ye be come unto Babylon, ye shall remain there many years, and for a long season, namely, seven generations: and after that I will bring you away

---

[67] [- *King James Bible "Authorized Version", Cambridge Edition*]

How the Bible Came To Us

peaceably from thence". Letter of Jeremiah 1:2-3 (- King James Bible "Authorized Version", Cambridge Edition)

This letter is purportedly a fictitious one, warning against idolatry, addressed to the Jews who were going to be led into Babylonian captivity. It sounds like literature intentionally created to win heathen over Jews who believed in Monotheism.

The writer of Epistle to Jeremiah was apparently from an imposter who intentionally ridiculed and his literature is filled with sarcasm.

"28. As for the things that are sacrificed unto them, their priests sell and abuse; in like manner their wives lay up part thereof in salt; but unto the poor and impotent they give nothing of it. 29 Menstruous women and women in childbed eat their sacrifices: by these things ye may know that they are no gods: fear them not. 30 For how can they be called gods? because women set meat before the gods of silver, gold, and wood". Letter to Jeremiah 1:28-30 ((- King James Bible "Authorized Version", Cambridge Edition)

A passage from the Old Testament Canonical Bible reads...

"But the LORD is the true God, he is the living God, and an everlasting king: at his wrath the earth shall tremble, and the nations shall not be able to abide his indignation. Thus shall ye say unto them, The gods that have not made the heavens and the earth, even they shall perish from the earth, and from under these heavens" (Jeremiah 10:10-11 KJV)

The Canonical Bible makes clear distinction between the living God and idols in dignified manner.

How the Bible Came To Us

PRAYER OF AZARIAH [68]

It is a fictitious song in prayer added after Daniel Chapter3:23 as if The Three Holy Children namely Shadrach, Meshach, and Abednego sang song to the LORD while they were in the furnace.

"And they walked in the midst of the fire, praising God, and blessing the Lord. 2 Then Azarias stood up, and prayed on this manner; and opening his mouth in the midst of the fire said, 3 Blessed art thou, O Lord God of our fathers: thy name is worthy to be praised and glorified for evermore" Prayer of Azariah[69] [- *King James Bible "Authorized Version", Cambridge Edition]*

The spurious insertion makes it appear as if there was a time delay for Christ in "Theophany" to be with Shadrach, Meshach, and Abednego, which if it was true, they would have been burnt alive; but in fact Nebuchadnezzar saw the fourth one in the midst of the fire.

The canonical Old Testament Daniel 3:23-24 read…

"And these three men, Shadrach, Meshach, and Abednego, fell down bound into the midst of the burning fiery furnace. Then Nebuchadnezzar the king was astonied, and rose up in haste, and spake, and said unto his counsellors, Did not we cast three men bound into the midst of the fire? They answered and said unto the king, True, O king" (Daniel 3:23-24)

---

[68] "Apocrapha Books" The Official King James Bible online n.d. Web[09 May, 2015]
[69] [- *King James Bible "Authorized Version", Cambridge Edition]*

SUSANNA

"vs. 44 And the Lord heard her voice. 45 therefore when she was led to be put to death, the Lord raised up the holy spirit of a young youth whose name was Daniel: 46 who cried with a loud voice, I am clear from the blood of this woman" Susanna Chapter 1:44-46

Daniel the wise man is reportedly received Holy Spirit and exposed the false testimony of two rapists, who made unlawful advances to Susanna, a beautiful and pious woman, to force her lie with them, but as she refused they turn to treacherous plan and make sure the she was branded by the council as adulteress . The text was a deliberate insertion to please the Jews in the Book of Daniel between Chapters 12 and 14 in the Septuagint version.

How the Bible Came To Us

BEL AND THE DRAGON

"3 Now the Babylons had an idol, called Bel, and there were spent upon him every day twelve great measures of fine flour, and forty sheep, and six vessels of wine. 4 And the king worshipped it and went daily to adore it: but Daniel worshipped his own God. And the king said unto him, Why dost not thou worship Bel? 5 Who answered and said, Because I may not worship idols made with hands, but the living God, who hath created the heaven and the earth, and hath sovereignty over all flesh. 6 Then said the king unto him, Thinkest thou not that Bel is a living God? seest thou not how much he eateth and drinketh every day? 7 Then Daniel smiled, and said, O king, be not deceived: for this is but clay within, and brass without, and did never eat or drink any thing. 8 So the king was wroth, and called for his priests, and said unto them, If ye tell me not who this is that devoureth these expences, ye shall die. 9 But if ye can certify me that Bel devoureth them, then Daniel shall die: for he hath spoken blasphemy against Bel. And Daniel said unto the king, Let it be according to thy word. Bel and the Dragon Chapter 1:3-9[70]

"27 Then Daniel took pitch, and fat, and hair, and did seethe them together, and made lumps thereof: this he put in the dragon's mouth, and so the dragon burst in sunder: and Daniel said, Lo, these are the gods ye worship. 28 When they of Babylon heard that, they took great indignation, and conspired against the king, saying, The king is become a Jew, and he hath destroyed Bel, he hath slain the dragon, and put the priests to death" Bel and the Dragon Chapter 1:27-28[71]

---

[70] - *King James Bible "Authorized Version", Cambridge Edition*
[71] - *King James Bible "Authorized Version", Cambridge Edition*

How the Bible Came To Us

Two stories that were not in the original Hebrew text were included in the Septuagint Greek version in about 150-100 BC of the book of Daniel. In the canonical Old Testament Bible which is based on the text from original Hebrew text Daniel's refusal to worship the idol set up by Persian King Darius does not say that he challenged their gods "Bel" and the "Dragon" by refusing to worship them or offer any sacrifice to them, but it only says Daniel prayed to God three times a day opening the window of his chamber facing east toward Jerusalem. He refused to obey the ordinance signed by the king that anyone who "shall ask a petition of any God or man for thirty days", except the king, he shall be cast into the den of lions. Daniel was triumphant in coming out of the den of lions because God closed the mouths of lions.

"Then these presidents and princes assembled together to the king, and said thus unto him, King Darius, live for ever. All the presidents of the kingdom, the governors, and the princes, the counsellors, and the captains, have consulted together to establish a royal statute, and to make a firm decree, that whosoever shall ask a petition of any God or man for thirty days, save of thee, O king, he shall be cast into the den of lions. Now, O king, establish the decree, and sign the writing, that it be not changed, according to the law of the Medes and Persians, which altereth not. Wherefore king Darius signed the writing and the decree". (Daniel 6:6-9)[72]

The story of Daniel throwing gauntlets at the king was in the Septuagint but not in the original Hebrew Text. The story of "Bel" narrates that Daniel refused give an offering to the idol saying that idol does not have mouth to eat. The priests, who

---

[72] The Holy Bible KJV

were commanded by the king to show how the idols ate the offering, go into the temple subtly through a secret door and eat the offering only to be caught red-handed by Daniel, who had spread ashes on the floor that caught the foot prints of the priests. The second story of the "Dragon" is of Daniel refusing to worship the dragon and challenging to kill it. He does it by feeding it a concoction of fat, hair and pitch. The dragon eats and dies. Daniel enemies, however, throw him into the den of lions, where lions were already fed their belly full by the prophet Habakkuk, who is brought there with enough food by the angels. Daniel is thrown into the den of lions and escapes the death. This was a fictional story included much later after the Persian rule.

THE PRAYER OF MANASSEH

King of Judah Manasseh did that which was evil in the sight of the LORD and God gave him over to King of Assyria who took him captive, by binding him with fetters, to Babylon. Manasseh in his affliction sought mercy from the LORD and the LORD forgave him. It was then that he became a true follower of God. (cf. 2 Chronicles 33:11-13; 33:15)

That is all the canonical Bible says, but someone added to the text the prayer of Manasseh which was not found in Hebrew Scriptures. This prayer was excellent, but it was a deliberate insertion in the original text to create some kind of sympathy towards Manasseh and also to show that God answers such prayer as that of Manasseh. It was, therefore, removed from the Bible.

The prayer of Manasseh:

How the Bible Came To Us

"O Lord, Almighty God of our fathers, Abraham, Isaac, and Jacob, and of their righteous seed; who hast made heaven and earth, with all the ornament thereof; who hast bound the sea by the word of thy commandment; who hast shut up the deep, and sealed it by thy terrible and glorious name; whom all men fear, and tremble before thy power; for the majesty of thy glory cannot be borne, and thine angry threatening toward sinners is importable: but thy merciful promise is unmeasurable and unsearchable; for thou art the most high Lord, of great compassion, longsuffering, very merciful, and repentest of the evils of men. Thou, O Lord, according to thy great goodness hast promised repentance and forgiveness to them that have sinned against thee: and of thine infinite mercies hast appointed repentance unto sinners, that they may be saved. Thou therefore, O Lord, that art the God of the just, hast not appointed repentance to the just, as to Abraham, and Isaac, and Jacob, which have not sinned against thee; but thou hast appointed repentance unto me that am a sinner: for I have sinned above the number of the sands of the sea. My transgressions, O Lord, are multiplied: my transgressions are multiplied, and I am not worthy to behold and see the height of heaven for the multitude of mine iniquities. I am bowed down with many iron bands, that I cannot lift up mine head, neither have any release: for I have provoked thy wrath, and done evil before thee: I did not thy will, neither kept I thy commandments: I have set up abominations, and have multiplied offences. Now therefore I bow the knee of mine heart, beseeching thee of grace. I have sinned, O Lord, I have sinned, and I acknowledge mine iniquities: wherefore, I humbly beseech thee, forgive me, O Lord, forgive me, and destroy me not with mine iniquites. Be not angry with me for ever, by reserving evil for me; neither condemn me to the lower parts of the earth. For thou art the God, even the God of them that repent; and in me thou wilt shew all thy goodness: for thou wilt save me, that am unworthy, according to thy great mercy. Therefore I will praise thee for ever all the days of my life: for all the powers of the heavens do praise thee, and thine is the glory for ever and ever. Amen". (*King James Bible "Authorized Version", Cambridge Edition*)

MACCABEES

"1 And it happened, after that Alexander son of Philip, the Macedonian, who came out of the land of Chettiim, had smitten Darius king of the Persians and Medes, that he reigned in his stead, the first over Greece, 2 And made many wars, and won many strong holds, and slew the kings of the earth, 3 And went through to the ends of the earth, and took spoils of many nations, insomuch that the earth was quiet before him; whereupon he was exalted and his heart was lifted up" I Maccabees 1:1-3 - *King James Bible "Authorized Version", Cambridge Edition)*

Flavius Josephus, the Jewish Historian writes in his book Antiq. XII Chapter 6 Para 1 that there was one by name Mattathias, who was the son of John, the son of Simeon, the son of "Asamoneus" (Hasmoneans), a citizen of Jerusalem. He had five sons, one of whom was Judas and he was Maccabeus.

Although the whole family of Judas has taken the title as "Maccabees" strictly speaking the name applies only to Judas. Maccabees, also known as Hasmoneans were very famous because of their revolt against Seleucid dynasty.

How the Bible Came To Us

Out of the four books of Maccabees only two are prominent, and other two are not so significant. These books are deuterocanonical books in the KJV 1611 edition.

The Books of the Maccabees are records of their life style, historical events from 175 BC to 134 BC, and related subjects. The books were written in Hebrew language, and St. Jerome, who translated the Bible into Latin vulgate, had seen those books; however the Hebrew text of Maccabees is now lost. Latin vulgate and KJV 1611 edition have only I Maccabees and II Maccabees but Septuagint has III and IV Maccabees also in addition to I and II Maccabees.

FIRST MACCABEES

A court historian of Hasmoneans is believed to have written the first book of Maccabees that deals primarily with the events of the rise of the Seleucid dynasty, history of the Jews, the desire of Antiochus to conquer Egypt, endeavors to suppress Jewish religion, Jewish rebellion, and many faithful Jews becoming martyrs. The details in the book were of high accuracy.

It presents the accurate account of political events and of Antiochus IV Epiphanies, who had set up Greek deity Zeus in the most Holy place of the Herod's Temple, and desecrated the temple by offering a pig as sacrifice to Zeus. Much later during Pauline times it was thought that Antiochus was the Antichrist, the man of sin, who was to come.

SECOND MACCABEES

Second Maccabees is not a continuation of first Maccabees but had a different account of the history events that happened during 161 B.C. This book focusses more on Judas Maccabaeus, and prayer for the dead in order that the dead may gain salvation. It was called "Purgatory".

According to dictionary purgatory is "(in the belief of Roman Catholics and others) a condition or place in which the souls of those dying penitent are purified from venial sins, or undergo the temporal punishment that, after the guilt of mortal sin has been remitted, still remains to be endured by the sinner". This is belief is considered by Protestant Christians as heresy. This book deals mainly with religious aspects of the Jews of Alexandria rather than political.

Such details of one family in large number of chapters, and their base being absent in the Jewish Hebrew Bible, the books of Maccabees were considered as mere historical and uninspired texts, and therefore, they did not find place in the Bible. Again, it was not human decision, but the decision of God who controlled the minds of the early Church Fathers who were instrumental in canonization of the whole Bible.

THIRD AND FOURTH MACCABEES

III Maccabees records persecution of Jews in 3rd century BC and 4th Maccabees records discourse praising the martyrs of Maccabees.

How the Bible Came To Us

CHAPTER 24
THE BANNED BOOKS

Just as we have millions of books of various categories in the Book shops, in the early days of Christianity there was huge literature in the form of books being circulated. No wonder the disciples of Jesus Christ and apostles suffered persecution at the hands of high priest and various other secular officials for propagating the Truth. If enemy can arise from within the Church, then there is no reason to believe that enemy with all his ferocity could arise from the world.

Those that arose from the world wrote much literature to counter the Scriptures with malicious intentions to defame Lord Jesus Christ and the true Scriptures. While some did to gain much importance in the world many did to discredit Christianity.

If entire literature was to be accommodated as the true scriptures then there would not have been a compendium of limited books in the Books in the Bible. It was hard for people to understand the truth about Christianity and the true God with all the malicious literature floating around in the early days after Lord Jesus Christ rose from the dead and ascended into heaven.

The Banned books were not recognized as the scriptures because the literature found in them was like that of fiction. It appears better than historians' writings inasmuch the latter write facts, while the former describes too many details to make the reading interesting.

How the Bible Came To Us

God's providence is greatly seen not only in the Old Testament to bring people to the knowledge of the truth by the mouths of prophets and by the decree of pagan, namely King Cyrus, to return the children of Israel to Jerusalem and rebuild the temple, the Lord's miraculous work was seen when He chose to work His way by the hand of a pagan emperor, whose name was Constantine.

Emperor Constantine of Roman Empire, according to legend had a vision in which he saw Cross and heard a voice that said to him to go ahead and conquer Maxentius at the "battle of the Milivian Bridge. Constantine fought the battle to victory. He built an imperial residence at Byzantium and renamed it as "Constantinople". Constantine's victory at the battle of the Milivian Bridge had influenced him to lean more towards Christianity rather than the Pagan beliefs he held until then.

UNCOMPROMSING STORIES

Some of the very disturbing stories found in the banned books raised questions as to whether or not Jesus killed another child when he was a boy, Mary Magdalene was a prostitute or an Apostle, did Cain committed incest, and does God is tricking men to believe that he shows His wrath during Apocalypse, were there jealous angels in the beginning, whether Satan refused to bow down to Adam, etc. There are no answers to such questions in the Bible and the stories had no source to believe, rendering them as mere fake stories and fictional interesting stories that would lead men astray from the Truth.

APOCRYPHAL BOOKS

The word "apocryphal" is different from "apocrypha", although some authors do not distinguish between these two terms. The

How the Bible Came To Us

text of apocrypha books is not found in the Hebrew Bible. The text of apocrypha books is found in Septuagint scattered in various sections. The said text was included in the Septuagint not for any reason, except for historical reasons, but found way into 1611 King James Bible in the form of 15 apocrypha books. The Authorized Version 1611 (KJV) placed these 15 books separately between the end of Old Testament and the New Testament, but were removed from later versions of the Bibles used by Protestants, who considered them as non-scriptures. They are still considered as scriptures by the Roman Catholics. Martin Luther considered them good for historical reasons but not for inclusion as Scriptures. The following are apocrypha books[73].

1. The First Book of Esdras
2. The Second Book of Esdras
3. Tobit
4. Judith
5. The Additions to the Book of Esther
6. The Wisdom of Solomon
7. Ecclesiasticus, or the Wisdom of Jesus the Son of Sirach
8. Baruch
9. The Letter of Jeremiah (This letter is sometimes incorporated as the last chapter of Baruch. When this is done the number of books is fourteen instead of fifteen.)
10. The Prayer of Azariah and the Song of the Three Young Men
11. Susanna
12. Bel and the Dragon
13. The Prayer of Manasseh
14. The First Book of Maccabees

---

[73] Apocrypha Books, The Official King James Bible online (The Authorized Version 1611 (KJV), n.d. web[07 June 2015])

How the Bible Came To Us

15. The Second Book of Maccabees

The main reason for considering apocrypha books as non-canonical is that the text of the said books was not found in the "Tanakh" (The Hebrew Old Testament). There are about 500 quotes in the New Testament that Jesus and apostles made to the Old Testament but none from the said books. Early Christians and Jews never considered them as inspired scriptures. The text is highly objectionable and shrouded with uncertainty, and dubious dating, and therefore, those fifteen books did not qualify as the inspired Scriptures.

There are about fifty gospels written after the resurrection of Jesus until 250 AD but only four made into the Canon. Those that did not make into the canon contained spurious, unsupported, fictitious material. The majority of such literature came from Marcion[74] and his Gnostic heretical followers. The most disturbing books that tried to malign the Biblical truths are the following banned books

1. The Life of Adam and Eve
2. The Book of Jubilees
3. The Books of Enoch
4. The Infancy Gospel of Thomas
5. The Gospel of Mary
6. The Book of Jasher
7. The Gospel of Judas
8. The Apocalypse of Peter

THE LIFE OF ADAM AND EVE

In Genesis account in Christian Bibles there are no extra details available as to the nature of temptation Eve suffered and about her fall which also led to Adam's fall than what is recorded which we read today. Holy Spirit decided the details made

---

[74] "The Gnostic Society Library" n.d. web[09 June 2015]

How the Bible Came To Us

available to us were enough for our inspiration, correction, and guidance. However, in the banned book, there are details that raise suspicion, such as jealous angels and a more vagrant serpent taking part and deceiving Eve are included. When such unacceptable fictitious stories are included it demands interrogation as to where the story is coming from, which community is part of creating such stories, or the author who wrote such story. At the end when it is discovered that they were fables added to induce believability the said books book become redundant. One such book is "THE LIFE OF ADAM AND EVE".

THE BOOK OF JUBILEES

It is strategy of enemy sometimes to give more details in addition to what is already there to convince people that the extra information given is legitimate. It just worked that way when enemy worked to write the names of the children of Adam and Eve and say Cain the eldest son of Adam married one of his sisters and call such relationship as incest. The enemy then plants wrong thoughts in the minds of innocents that Bible is not true.

Eve is created by God from the rib of Adam and it is no sin for Adam and Eve to have husband and wife relationship. The law forbidding marriages among close relatives is not given by God until the children of Israel were in the wilderness travelling from Egypt to Canaan. Why does it matter for man to consider it 'incest' when God commanded Adam and Eve to replenish the earth and fill the earth with their children? What gives the power to be judgmental for those who propagate the idea that brother and sister relationship as that of husband and wife in

How the Bible Came To Us

the beginning until the law was given prohibiting such relationship was in error; are they above God?

Here is what the book of Jubilees says...

"...And Cain took Awan his sister to be his wife and she bare him Enoch at the close fo the fourth jubilee..." The Book of Jubilees 4:9

The Inspired Scriptures does not name Cain's wife but records the lineage as follows:

"And Adam lived an hundred and thirty years, and begat a son in his own likeness, after his image; and called his name Seth: And the days of Adam after he had begotten Seth were eight hundred years: and he begat sons and daughters: And all the days that Adam lived were nine hundred and thirty years: and he died" (Genesis 5:3-5)

Thus even though Cain's wife seems to be enigmatic being, she could be either his sister or cousin; notwithstanding such marriage was not incest inasmuch as no such was law was given by God to treat it as incest. Abraham married his half-sister and such relationship was considered as sin until after four hundred years passed.

"And yet indeed she is my sister; she is the daughter of my father, but not the daughter of my mother; and she became my wife" (Genesis 20:12)

In addition to the above example there are many other inconsistencies in the Book of Jubilees that makes it a banned book.

How the Bible Came To Us

THE BOOK OF ENOCH

The Book of Enoch contains story of angels of about two hundred of them who rebelled against God and have fallen from His grace went out to earth and had illicit sexual relationship with the daughters of men as quipped in Genesis chapter 6 account. The Bible does not give details as to who the 'sons of God' were who went into the 'daughters of men'. The popular belief among Christians is that Bible refers angels as 'sons of God' in the book of Job, and therefore, a conjecture is made that the fallen angels were the 'sons of God'. The angels are spirits and even though they could take the form of men, they have no flesh, bones and blood in them, and therefore, the conjecture made that they would have had sexual relationship with the daughters of men was unacceptable by section of Christians. The angels that did not rebel against God and did not do such sin went to God, according to the Book of Enoch, and complained to God about the fallen angels' sin. Therefore, according to the said book, the fallen angels were bound in chains and put in prison. Another inconsistency of this book is that Sheba the queen went to King Solomon and not only praised him and presented gifts to him but also she brought back in her womb the seed of Solomon, and as the Ethiopians believed for many centuries, was the first Ethiopian king. The stories seemed to be concocted because there was no continuity them in the fragments found by Scholars or in the Dead Sea scrolls that were discovered much later. This is the reason why this book was banned from the Bible.

THE GOSPEL OF THOMAS

Someone made a cunning move as an imposter to malign the name of Jesus Christ by introducing stories that never were

How the Bible Came To Us

true. Was it Thomas, disciple of Jesus, who wrote this book; apparently not. The writer projects Jesus as a violent man, who killed someone of his age when he was of his age and suddenly paints Him as one who had compassion to resurrect him. The childhood of Jesus from his age 12 until He took up the ministry when He was of 30 years of age is shrouded in mystery. This book contains 114 sayings purportedly of Jesus; but they all seemed to be controversial and of base reading, and therefore it was concluded that Jesus would never have said those sayings. The Bible does not record His life during these days; but the literature that came up within 100 years of Jesus' resurrection records it. There are more disturbing incidences of His life with no authority of reliability are recorded in this book, and therefore, this book is banned from the Bible. This book fails to meet all the four principles set forth to recognize if a book is genuine. Those principles were to see if the author was an apostle, or if he had any close connection with an apostle, was the book accepted generally by the body of Christ, did the book consistent in doctrine and did the book depict high moral and spiritual values.

THE PROTOVANGELION OF JAMES

The details presented by the Gospel writers, as guided by the Holy Spirit, in our Bibles about Virgin Mary are solemn, and she is revered as the earthly mother of Jesus; nothing more and nothing less. She, as a mother of Jesus, was not exempt from accepting Jesus as Lord. The Word became flesh in the form of a servant in the likeness of man, born of the Virgin Mary, "conceived in her is of the Holy Ghost". (Matthew 1:20b), and that child who grew up, was the Lord of all, including that of Mary, who gave birth to the Jesus.

How the Bible Came To Us

The protovangelion of James, however, presents more details than were found in the inspired Scriptures. Some spurious documents, perhaps from someone with pseudonym, came up portraying the details of her birth, of her parents, of her youth and venerating her above Lord Jesus Christ in order to render to her the worship that is due to the Lord. The book falls short of the demands of the inspired Scriptures which say...

"Thou shalt have no other gods before me" (Exodus 20:3)

"Jesus said unto him, Thou shalt love the Lord thy God with all thy heart, and with all thy soul, and with all thy mind" (Matthew 22:37)

"THE PROTOVANGELION OF JAMES" did not meet requirement that needed to be included in the Bible, and therefore, it was banned from the Bible.

THE GOSPEL OF MARY MAGDALENE

Gnostic views penetrated the Church powerfully in order to divert Christians from salvation by grace through faith. Mary Magdalene was a good believer and she is saved by grace through faith; nothing more and nothing less. It is not by her gaining the knowledge of the secret of salvation, or by seeing a vision as to how her soul or of her savior that travels through the third heaven, surpassing the so-called power of ignorance that she was saved. It is simple faith in Jesus Christ and accepting Him as Lord that saved her.

"The Gospel of Mary" of which several pages are missing is a book filled with Gnostic views that undermine the deity of Lord Jesus Christ. It presents Jesus as a mere prophet similar to any other prophet who lived before Him. This book is written by anonymous writer, and it has several lies, myths and blasphemes. It leads common and simple men into deception and misguides them. It shows as if Mary Magdalene not as a prostitute but as an apostle. The text in this book has already poisoned the Church with divisions and debates about the role of women in the Church, and as to why they should cover their heads, and as to why they should not be preachers, etc.

Lord Jesus Christ is the only Savior and no one comes to the Father but by Him. Gnostic texts open up simple believers into confusions and deception. Confess by mouth that Jesus as Lord and believe in heart that God raised Him from the dead on the third day and that is the only way for one to receive salvation and not perish.

"Jesus saith unto him, I am the way, the truth, and the life: no man cometh unto the Father, but by me" (John 14:6)

Jesus said: "I and my Father are one" (John 10:30)

"For God so loved the world, that he gave his only begotten Son, that whosoever believeth in him should not perish, but have everlasting life" (John 3:16)

THE GOSPEL OF NICODEMUS

GOSPEL OF NICODEMUS

Gospel of Nicodemus, the source of which is not known, is a banned book of the Bible. The reading of the text of this book is so debased that it rightly deserves to be banned. There are three sections in this book. The first section deals with the trial of Jesus before Pilate. The points of the text in all possibility are a stolen text from Luke 23 and modified to suit the heresy and falsehood to misguide the believers. The trial is argumentative

How the Bible Came To Us

and does not read like spiritual text. The miracles Jesus did are debated. The second section deals with the so-called descent of Jesus to hell to preach Gospel to the imprisoned spirits and manhandles Satan and hands him over to Hades. The third section deals the so-called ascent of Jesus from hell and brings out the Old Testament saints. (Unfortunately, some Christians so deceived by this text they could not discern the truth but teach this doctrine as true).

Excerpts[75] from Gospel of Nicodemus are as follows:

CHAP. XIX.

11 Then the Lord stretching forth his hand, made the sign of the cross upon Adam, and upon all his saints. 12 And taking hold of Adam by his right hand, he ascended from hell, and all the saints of God followed him.13 Then the royal prophet David boldly cried, and said, 1 O sing unto the Lord a new song, for he hath done marvellous things; his right hand and his holy arm have gotten him the victory.14 The Lord hath made known his salvation, his righteousness hath he openly shewn in the sight of the heathen.15 And the whole multitude of saints answered, saying, 2 This honour have all his saints, Amen, Praise ye the Lord.16 Afterwards, the prophet Habakkuk 3 cried out, and said, Thou wentest forth for the salvation of thy people, even for the salvation of thy people.17 And all the saints said, 4 Blessed is he who cometh in the name of the Lord; for the Lord hath enlightened us. This is our God for ever and ever; he shall reign over us to everlasting ages, Amen.18 In like manner all the prophets spake the sacred things of his praise, and followed the Lord.

---

[75] Gospel of Nicodemus text is in Public Domain (published prior to 1922).

How the Bible Came To Us

CHAP. XVI

11 And I said in another place, O death, where is thy victory? O death, where is thy sting? 12 When all the saints heard these things spoken by Isaiah, they said to the prince of hell, 1 Open now thy gates, and take away thine iron bars; for thou wilt now be bound, and have no power. 13 Then there was a great voice, as of the sound of thunder saying, Lift up your gates, O princes; and be ye lifted up, ye gates of hell, and the King of Glory will enter in. 14 The prince of hell perceiving the same voice repeated, cried out as though he had been ignorant, Who is that King of Glory? 15 David replied to the prince of hell, and said, I understand the words of that voice, because I spake them by his spirit. And now, as I have above said, I say unto thee, the Lord strong and powerful, the Lord mighty in battle: he is the King of Glory, and he is the Lord in heaven and in earth; 16 He hath looked down to hear the groans of the prisoners, and to set loose those that are appointed to death. 17 And now, thou filthy and stinking prince of hell, open thy gates, that the King of Glory may enter in; for he is the Lord of heaven and earth. 18 While David was saying this, the mighty Lord appeared in the form of a man, and enlightened those places which had ever before been in darkness, 19 And broke asunder the fetters which before could not be broken; and with his invincible power visited those who sate in the deep darkness by iniquity, and the shadow of death by sin.

CHAP. XVIII[76]

7 O Satan, thou prince of all the wicked, father of the impious and abandoned, why wouldest thou attempt this exploit, seeing our prisoners were hitherto always without the least hopes of

---

[76] Gospel of Nicodemus text is in Public Domain (published prior to 1922).

How the Bible Came To Us

salvation and life? 8 But now there is not one of them does ever groan, nor is there the least appearance of a tear in any of their faces. 9 O prince Satan, thou great keeper of the infernal regions, all thy advantages which thou didst acquire by the forbidden tree, and the loss of Paradise, thou hast now lost by the wood of the cross; 10 And thy happiness all then expired, when thou didst crucify Jesus Christ the King of Glory. 11 Thou hast acted against thine own interest and mine, as thou wilt presently perceive by those large torments and infinite punishments which thou art about to suffer. 12 O Satan, prince of all evil, author of death, and source of all pride, thou shouldest first have inquired into the evil crimes of Jesus of Nazareth, and then thou wouldest have found that he was guilty of no fault worthy of death. 13 Why didst thou venture, without either reason or justice, to crucify him, and hast brought down to our regions a person innocent and righteous, and thereby hast lost all the sinners, impious and unrighteous persons in the whole world? 14 While the prince of hell was thus speaking to Satan, the King of Glory said to Beelzebub, the prince of hell, Satan, the prince shall be subject to thy dominion for ever, in the room of Adam and his righteous sons, who are mine.

THE APOCALYPSE OF PETER

The meaning of "apocalypse" is any of a class of Jewish or Christian writings that appeared from about 200 B.C. to A.D. 350 and were assumed to make revelations of the ultimate divine purpose. (Dictionary[77])

There are two apocalypses. One is from Peter, supposedly written by Apostle Peter, and another from John. The text of

---

[77] "apocalypse." Dictionary.com Unabridged. Random House, Inc. 10 Jun. 2015.

How the Bible Came To Us

the apocalypse of peter shows that it is not divinely inspired text and the author seems to have been a pirate or imposter. The said apocalypse shows that God is extremely good and therefore, He would not allow anyone to be in hell. It suggests that any evil doer can get out of hell either by asking forgiveness from hell or at the discretion of God and the threat of hell or punishment in hell is to scare men in order that they may live a holy and moral life.

On the contrary John's apocalypse known as "Revelation" explains the true nature of God that He will punish evil doers and give rewards to those who obey and follow Him. Eternity is extremely good for those who are saved by the precious blood of Lord Jesus Christ, who paid the price of our sins. Everyone who believes that Jesus is Lord and believes in heart that God raised Him from the dead will be saved from perishing and suffering in the "lake of fire" which is prepared for evil-doers.

CHAPTER 25
NEW TESTAMENT CANON

THE NEW TESTAMENT [78]

The following are the most widely accepted dates[79], authors, classification of the New Testament books[80]

	BOOK	WRITTEN IN	AUTHOR	CLASSIFICATION
1.	Gospel according to Matthew	70-110 AD	Matthew	Synoptic Gospel
2.	Gospel according to Mark	60-70 AD	Mark	Synoptic Gospel
3.	Gospel according to Luke	60-70 AD	Luke	Synoptic Gospel
4.	Gospel according to John	80-95 AD	John	Gospel of Jesus Christ
5.	Acts	60-90 AD	Luke	Historical
6.	Romans	56 AD	Paul	Epistolary
7.	1 Corinthians	54 AD	Paul	Epistolary
8.	2 Corinthians	56 AD	Paul	Epistolary
9.	Galatians	45-55 AD	Paul	Epistolary

---

[78] David E. Aune(Edited).The Blackwell Companion to the New Testament
[79] Raymond E. Brown, an Introduction to the New Testament, Anchor Bible, 1997. pp. 456-466.
[80] Evans, Craig A. (2008). "Introduction". In Evans. Craig A. Tov, Emanuel. Exploring the Origins of the Bible: Canon Formation in Historical, Literary, and Theological Perspective

How the Bible Came To Us

10. Ephesians	61-62 AD	Paul	Epistolary
11. Philippians	61–62 AD	Paul	Epistolary
12. Colossians	61-62 AD	Paul	Epistolary
13. 1 Thessalonians	51-52 AD	Paul	Epistolary
14. 2 Thessalonians	51-54 AD	Paul	Epistolary
15. 1 Timothy	61-62 AD	Paul	Epistolary
16. 2 Timothy	63 AD	Paul	Epistolary
17. Titus	62-64 AD	Paul	Epistolary
18. Philemon	60 AD	Paul	Epistolary
19. Hebrews	63-90 AD	Paul[81]	General Epistle[82]
20. James	50-200 AD	James	General Epistle
21. 1 Peter	60-96 AD	Peter	General Epistle
22. 2 Peter	60-130 AD	Peter	General Epistle
23. 1 John	90-110 AD	John	General Epistle
24. 2 John	90-110 AD	John	General Epistle
25. 3 John	90-110 AD	John	General Epistle
26. Jude	66-90 AD	Jude	General Epistle

---

[81] Authorship is disputed, yet most scholars accept that Paul is the Author of Hebrews

[82] Authorship is disputed, yet most scholars accept that Paul is the Author of Hebrews

How the Bible Came To Us

| 27. Revelation | 68-100 AD | John | Apocalypse |

"These things God has revealed to us through the Spirit. For the Spirit searches everything, even the depths of God. For who knows a person's thoughts except the spirit of that person, which is in him? So also no one comprehends the thoughts of God except the Spirit of God. Now we have received not the spirit of the world, but the Spirit who is from God, that we might understand the things freely given us by God. And we impart this in words not taught by human wisdom but taught by the Spirit, interpreting spiritual truths to those who are spiritual (1 Corinthians 2:10-13 ESV)

It is God who decided what should be in the Bible and what should not be. The New Testament contains the Word of God just as the Old Testament does. The Church Fathers have put in many years of hard labor for the Lord, and discovered the text that was inspired by God. They did not decide what should be in the Bible but they were spiritually guided by God as to what should be included and to remove unscrupulous text that was circulated by enemies of God.

The Scripture says in the mouth of two or three witnesses a matter can be settled and in the case of canonization of the Bible not one or two but several Church elders decided the number of books and the text that should be in the Bible. The text that was in the form of fragments was gathered by scholars over several and it was, the number of words counted and in the process codex was compiled first.

According to the will of God the New Testament was put alongside the Old Testament God's inspired scripture. Holy

How the Bible Came To Us

Spirit guided them and controlled their actions and minds to make available the scripture as the Father decided. The Bible is His word and not man's word.

CHAPTER 26
APOSTLE PAUL'S MISSIONARY WORK

POINTS IN CONCISE

1. Paul, who is born of Tarsus, Cilicia, and a Hebrew, of the tribe of Benjamin, Pharisee, and a Roman Citizen by birth, is converted on the Road to Damascus (cf. Acts 9:1-9). [Earlier, he consented the stoning of Stephen to death, and persecuted the church].
2. He goes to Damascus to meet Ananias and is anointed (cf. Acts 9:10-19).
3. Travels to Arabia and remains there (Gal 1:17).
4. Returns to Damascus then leaves the city for safety (Gal 1:17; Acts 9:20-25; 2 Cor. 11:32-33).
   Travels to Jerusalem (cf. Acts 9:26-29; Gal 1:18).
5. Travels back to Tarsus for safety (cf. Acts 9:30); [Barnabas travels to Tarsus in order to seek Saul (cf. Acts 11:25)].
6. Travels along with Barnabas to Antioch preaching God's Word(cf. Acts 11:26).
7. Saul[83] and Barnabas return with John Mark (cf. Acts 12:25).
8. Saul and Barnabas "separated" for Lord's work and sent out (cf. Acts 13:2. 3).

FIRST MISSIONARY JOURNEY

9. They leave Antioch for Seleucia, then to Cyprus (cf. Acts 13:4).
10. While on their way to Cyprus they visit Salamis and Paphos (cf. Acts 13:5-12).
11. From Paphos they travel to Perga of Pamphylia and it is at this place that a major event takes place; John Mark

---

[83] Names and "Paul" and "Saul" are used interchangeably. Paul's name was "Saul" before conversion and the name "Paul" was not used until Acts 13:9

How the Bible Came To Us

departs for home, and it becomes reason for contention (cf. Acts 13:13; Acts 15:36-41).
12. Paul ministers in Antioch of Pisidia (cf. Acts 13:14-50).
13. He is at Iconium (cf. Acts 13:51 - 14:6).
14. Paul travels to Lystra and Derbe, preaching the Gospel of Jesus Christ (cf. Acts 14:6-7).
15. People in Lystra mistake Paul and Barnabas for gods. They called Barnabas, Jupiter; and Paul, Mercurius (cf. Acts 14:8-18).
16. They were stoned at Lystra and people suppose they were dead, but surprisingly they reenter the city (cf. Acts 14:19-20).
17. Paul with Barnabas leave for Derbe, preaching the Gospel of Jesus Christ (cf. Acts 14:20-21).
18. They return to Lystra. Iconium, and Antioch and not only strengthen disciples but appoint elders (cf. Acts 14:21-24).
19. From Pisidia they return to Antioch of Syria. They report about their journey to the church (cf. Acts 14:24-28).
20. Paul and Barnabas dispute with certain false teachers and reason with them at the Jerusalem Council (cf. Acts 15:1-29; Galatians 2:1).
21. Paul and Barnabas return to Antioch of Syria preaching the Gospel of Jesus Christ(cf. Acts 15:30-35; Galatians 2:11-14).
22. Paul and Barnabas have serious contention over John Mark and they part ways for good. Barnabas and John Mark sail to Cyprus (cf. Acts 15:36-39).

SECOND MISSIONARY JOURNEY

23. Paul and Silas depart. They go via Syria and Cilicia strengthening the churches (cf. Acts 15:40-41).
24. They travel to Derbe and Lystra and pick up Timotheus, strengthening the churches (cf. Acts 16:1-5).
25. They travel to Troas. Paul sees Macedonian in a vision (cf. Acts 16:6-10).

26. They sail from Troas to Neapolis (cf. Acts 16:11).
27. Then they travel to Philippi. Paul meets Lydia, a seller of purple, of the city of Thyatira. (cf. Acts 16:12-15).
28. Paul and Silas imprisoned after casting out evil spirit from a slave girl (cf. Acts 16:16-25).
29. Prison doors open miraculously and the jailer saved (cf. Acts 16:25-34).
30. They depart from Philippi (cf. Acts 16:35-40).
31. They pass through Amphipolis and Apollonia (cf. Acts 17:1).
32. They preach Jesus Christ at Thessalonica and had to leave (cf. Acts 17:1-10).
33. They were at Berea where Paul leaves Silas and Timothy (cf. Acts 17:10-14).
34. Silas and Timothy join Paul at Corinth. (cf. Acts 18:1-17).
35. Paul stops at Ephesus, Caesarea and Jerusalem while returning to Antioch (cf. Acts 18:18-22).

THIRD MISSIONARY JOURNEY

36. They travels through Galatia and Phrygia and strengthen the disciples in Spirit (cf. Acts 18:23).
37. They travel via upper regions whey on their way to Ephesus (cf. Acts 19:1).
38. They do the Lord's ministry in Ephesus (cf. Acts 19:1-41).
39. They travel to Macedonia (cf. Acts 20:1).
40. And then they travel to Greece (cf. Acts 20:2).
41. They travel back to Macedonia (cf. Acts 20:3).
42. They were at Troas (cf. Acts 20:4-12). Assos. Mitylene. Chios. Samos. Togyllium. (cf. Acts 20:13-15).
43. When they were at Miletus Paul exhorts the Ephesian elders (cf. Acts 20:15-38).
44. They were at Coos. Rhodes. Patara. Phoenicia. (cf. Acts 21:1. 2).
45. At Tyre (cf. Acts 21:3-6). At Ptolemais (cf. Acts 21:7).
46. At Caesarea (cf. Acts 21:8-14).

How the Bible Came To Us

47. At Jerusalem (cf. Acts 21:15-25).
48. Paul is arrested in the temple and causes an uproar (cf. Acts 21:26-36).
49. Paul addresses the mob (cf. Acts 21:37 - 22:21).
50. Paul's Roman citizenship by birth saves him from being scourged (cf. Acts 22:22-29).
51. He faces the Council (also called the "Sanhedrin") (cf. Acts 22:30 - 23:10).
52. Lord Jesus appears to Paul and tells Paul that the latter will bear witness for him in Rome (cf. Acts 23:11).
53. Some forty or more Jews conspire to kill Paul (cf. Acts 23:12-22).
54. Paul is sent by Chief Captain Claudius safely to Felix the governor (cf. Acts 23:23-35).
55. Paul defends himself before Felix, but Felix keeps him in custody for two years and hands him over to his successor Festus (cf. Acts 24:1-27).
56. Paul defends himself before Festus the governor (cf. Acts 25:1-12).

JOURNEY TO ROME

57. Paul's appeal to have his case adjudicated at Caesar's court in Rome and his plea is honored – It was a turning point and he ventures towards Rome (cf. Acts 25:12).
58. Paul stands before Agrippa (cf. Acts 25:13 - 26:32).
59. Paul leaves for Rome and then sails to Myra (cf. Acts 27:1-5).
60. They continue their sailing and reach "Fair Havens" on Crete (cf. Acts 27:6-8).
61. The captain of the ship and sailors venture sailing in spite of Paul's warning against it. (cf. Acts 27:9-12).
62. They were all caught in the midst of a huge storm their ship wrecks. They reach the island of Malta by swimming or on wrecked parts of the ship (cf. Acts 27:13 - 28:1).
63. Paul is at Malta (cf. Acts 28:2-10).

64. He sails to Syracuse (cf. Acts 28:11. 12).
65. Then he sails to Rhegium then Puteoli (cf. Acts 28:13).

PAUL'S FIRST ROMAN IMPRISONMENT

66. Paul arrives in Rome (cf. Acts 28:14-16).
67. Paul meets the Jews (cf. Acts 28:17-28).
68. He preaches the Gospel of Jesus Christ for two full years, without hindrance, in his rented house (cf. Acts 28:30-31).
69. Paul is released from Roman imprisonment
70. He does further missionary work

PAUL'S SECOND ROMAN IMPRISONMENT

71. Paul dies as martyr under Nero according to secular history.

How the Bible Came To Us

CHAPTER 27
CANONIZATION OF THE BIBLE[84]

Canon means:

1. An ecclesiastical rule or law enacted by a council or other competent authority and, in the Roman Catholic Church, approved by the pope.
2. The books of the Bible recognized by any Christian church as genuine and inspired.

Gospel writers Matthew and Luke mentioned about Lord Jesus Christ's reference to Hebrew Scripture as the "Law of Moses", "the Prophets", and "the Psalms". This is very unique about the New Testament Canon. Not only the phrase "it is written" occurs in the Old Testament but it occurs very often in the New Testament. The Scripture substantiates scripture; and this is very unique in the Bible.

These are the words of Lord Jesus Christ quoting from 2 Chronicles 24:20-22, as to how the children of Israel killed the prophets.

"That upon you may come all the righteous blood shed upon the earth, from the blood of righteous Abel unto the blood of Zacharias son of Barachias, whom ye slew between the temple and the altar" (Matthew 23:35)

"From the blood of Abel unto the blood of Zacharias, which perished between the altar and the temple: verily I say unto you, It shall be required of this generation" (Luke 11:51)

---

[84] Athanasius Letter 39.6.3: "Let no man add to these, neither let him take ought from these." n.d. Web [05 May, 2015]

How the Bible Came To Us

"And he said unto them, These are the words which I spake unto you, while I was yet with you, that all things must be fulfilled, which were written in the law of Moses, and in the prophets, and in the psalms, concerning me" (Luke 24:44)

Lord Jesus spoke of His anointing and His ministry by reading a scripture portion from the Old Testament repeated in New Testament.

"The Spirit of the Lord is upon me, because he hath anointed me to preach the gospel to the poor; he hath sent me to heal the brokenhearted, to preach deliverance to the captives, and recovering of sight to the blind, to set at liberty them that are bruised" (Luke 4:18).

"The Spirit of the Lord GOD is upon me; because the LORD hath anointed me to preach good tidings unto the meek; he hath sent me to bind up the brokenhearted, to proclaim liberty to the captives, and the opening of the prison to them that are bound; (Isaiah 61:1)

Lord Jesus referred to Hebrew Scriptures in Luke 11:51, Matthew 23:35, and further identified them in Luke 24:44, as the Law, the Prophets and the Psalms. His identification marks a clear demarcation between the Old and the New Testaments.

Inasmuch as He was alive and was on His mission, the New Testament, which is about Him and His works, and His provision for salvation to mankind, was not yet written. He recognized Hebrew Scriptures written up to Malachi in 425 BC as Scripture.

The Bible was canonized with thirty nine books of the Hebrew Scripture and twenty seven books of the New Testament by the end of 397 A.D. Inasmuch as Hebrew believers recognized the

How the Bible Came To Us

Hebrew Scripture as inspired Word of God, there was very little controversy over the canonization of the Old Testament and therefore, Old Testament was canonized by 250 A.D.

However there was much debate as to how many books should be in the New Testament and what books should be therein. The emerging issue that created much controversy was over the "Apocrypha" which had very good historical evidence, but not spiritual in content.

How the Bible Came To Us

CHAPTER 28
THE DEVELOPMENT

LEADING TO NEW TESTAMENT CANON

The New Testament did not come into being all of a sudden nor was it formed at the Nicaea Council; but rather it was a gradual development. The decisions taken at Nicaea Council was neither to define God nor was it for formation of the Bible. The decision taken there was to see Christians have uniformity in interpretation as to who Jesus was and to have the Scriptures into Codex (into a Book format).

The early Christians already had the Hebrew Bible called "Old Testament" in their hands and they rather suffered persecutions than give up the Scriptures. The missionary movements included their travel to foreign lands and then there was the need to have the papyri into codex.

The scriptures accepted to the be in the codex should have had the authority of God just as Jesus said "it is written" and should have fulfilled the demand as He said…"… These are the words which I spake unto you, while I was yet with you, that all things must be fulfilled, which were written in the Law of Moses, and in the prophets, and in the psalms, concerning me" (Luke 24:44)

Or for example as apostles said: "Paul, a servant of Jesus Christ, called to be an apostle, separated unto the gospel of God" (Romans 1:1)

Or, "Peter, an apostle of Jesus Christ, to the strangers scattered throughout Pontus, Galatia, Cappadocia, Asia, and Bithynia, Elect according to the foreknowledge of God the Father,

How the Bible Came To Us

through sanctification of the Spirit, unto obedience and sprinkling of the blood of Jesus Christ: Grace unto you, and peace, be multiplied" (1 Peter 1:1-2) etc.

Or should have apostolic authority such as apostle Peter authorized Mark to write the Gospel of Mark, Paul authorized Luke to write the Gospel of Luke and Acts of Apostles, and should have been of Universal acceptance by Jewish Community of the Old Testament period, and and should have Consistent message devoid of contradictory material.

In the 1st and 2nd century the Scriptures were translated into Syriac, Old Latin and in the 3rd century into Coptic (Egyptian Christians were called "Coptic Christians"). The Church was built upon "...the foundation of the apostles and prophets, Jesus Christ himself being the chief corner stone" (Ephesians 2:20)

The three phase development was clearly evident in the determination of Canon.

1. The first phase was from Apostolic age to 170 AD
2. The second phase was from 170 AD to 220 AD
3. The Third phase was from 3rd to 4th Century.

Important people involved, in the decision making to have a volume or call it codex or call it book, were Clement of Rome, Ignatius, Polycarp, Irenaeus, Origen, Dionysius, Cyprian, Eusebius, Athanasius, Jerome, Augustine, Martin Luther. Besides them there was one who practiced Gnosticism and he was Marcion, a Bishop, who wrote heresy and he and his writings were banned. Marcion's heretical views and Arian heresy from Arius provoked the true followers of Jesus Christ to counter them in their views. The forces which influenced were the Council of Nicaea and the council of Carthage.

How the Bible Came To Us

CLEMENT OF ROME

The first phase was from apostolic age to 170 AD, when Clement of Rome, Ignatius, and Polycarp were great instruments in the development Christianity preaching from the New Testament books that were yet to be formed into one book.

Clement was an elder, whom Roman Catholics called as Pope Clement I, propagated Christianity vehemently. Forty years after Paul wrote his two letters to Corinthians, Clement wrote in AD 96 to the Church at Corinth, indicating to us that Corinthians repented of their divisive attitude and returning for unification on great ideals Paul taught them.

This age from Jesus to AD 170 was of the development of New Testament with the life history of Jesus, His teachings and His stand as mediator between God and man, His substitutionary death, burial, resurrection and ascension to be seated on the right hand of the Majesty, and His promise of sending the Comforter to be in us and with us, and the promise of His second coming.

Apostles and others appointed by the apostles were very actively involved in proclaiming the Gospel of Jesus Christ. Apostle Paul, who was Saul before his conversion, persecuted the Church, but when Lord Jesus encountered him, he remorsefully repented of what he had done, and then spent his whole life time for Lord Jesus Christ. There were also others who were with him or were present during his time who took much interest in proclaiming the Gospel.

Before the commencement of the 2nd Century all the New Testament books were in existence. The four Gospels of the

How the Bible Came To Us

New Testament books contain the details of the birth of Jesus, His ministry on the earth, and His death, burial, resurrection and ascension. Other books are epistles, and individual letters and the book of Revelation.

The New Testament was given to the Church and the Church considered as the treasure of the Word of God. Lord Jesus came into the world in the form of servant and in the likeness of man, and He was and is God and, therefore, He can forgive sins. Apostle Paul, who considered himself as a bond servant of Lord Jesus Christ wrote...

"Therefore let us not sleep, as do others; but let us watch and be sober. For they that sleep sleep in the night; and they that be drunken are drunken in the night. But let us, who are of the day, be sober, putting on the breastplate of faith and love; and for an helmet, the hope of salvation. For God hath not appointed us to wrath, but to obtain salvation by our Lord Jesus Christ" (1 Thessalonians 5:6-9)

"And when this epistle is read among you, cause that it be read also in the church of the Laodiceans; and that ye likewise read the epistle from Laodicea" (Colossians 4:16)

POLYCARP

Polycarp (70-155 AD), who was a contemporary of Ignatius, was one of the prominent bishops of the early church, and a disciple of Apostle John, and a teacher of Irenaeus. He was an arch connecting figure of biblical apostles and the age of early church leaders. Many documents from old sources, including his letters to the church at Philippi, project him as ardent lover of Christ. He greatly encouraged the church at Philippi to flee from worldly pleasures and remain strong in faith.

How the Bible Came To Us

Irenaeus, his student who was also one of the leaders of the early church, wrote that Polycarp had instructions from the apostles of Jesus Christ and from Apostle John and accordingly was brought into contact with many believers of Jesus Christ. After standing true to the Lord, Polycarp was martyred by the Romans. His martyrdom brought great revolution among the pagans.

Polycarp, who was the bishop of the church at Smyrna, successfully combated heresies among Christians. Marcion was one of the leaders of heretics, who brought significant damage to the beliefs of Christianity. It is said that one of the colleagues of Marcion called him as the firstborn of Satan. Such great was the heresy he spread creating his own bible and making serious endeavors to damage Christianity. Polycarp and others like Athanasius, who was a staunch believer in Jesus Christ, had tough time combating Marcion. Nevertheless, the truth triumphed ultimately.

It was evident from Polycarp's martyrdom and those of other disciples; God's intervention in the lives of men was different from that of Old Testament saints. Daniel, Shadrach, Meshach and Abednego felt the presence of the Lord. They refused to worship the kings and their ordinances and when they were subjected to severe punishment, such as Daniel being thrown into lion's den, and other three being thrown into fiery furnace, at different time intervals, others saw Jesus in Christophany with them and they did not die instantly. However, in the New Testament period, every disciple of Jesus Christ became martyr, and Polycarp was no exception.

The emperors of Rome persecuted Christians much more than the high priests and others who persecuted Apostle Paul and his

How the Bible Came To Us

associates during the Acts of the Apostle period. Those early leaders who endeavored to bring fruit in the vineyard of Lord Jesus Christ suffered and were martyred. Poly carp was asked to confess and proclaim "Caesar is my Lord". The early church leaders knew what Paul taught and it was...

"That if thou shalt confess with thy mouth the Lord Jesus, and shalt believe in thine heart that God hath raised him from the dead, thou shalt be saved. For with the heart man believeth unto righteousness; and with the mouth confession is made unto salvation" (Romans 10:9-10)

Polycarp without any hesitation refused to confess and proclaim "Caesar is my Lord" but boldly said "Eighty-six years I have served Christ, and He never did me any wrong. How can I blaspheme my King who saved me?" He was steadfast in his beliefs in Christ and stood for the Lord. The result was that Caesar's anger burnt against him and Polycarp was burnt alive to death at the Stake.

Polycarp's letter to the church at Philippi was quite noteworthy and had much significance in the progress of Christianity in the first phase after the Acts of apostle's period. Firstly, it emphasized on the necessity of giving credence to Christ's and Paul's teachings and stand against heresies. Secondly, his letter contained many paraphrases from the texts that later became four Gospels, and letters of Paul to Philippians, Thessalonians, to Timothy, and letters of Peter, John and Jude. His references to these books and letters gave much ground to distinguish inspired scriptures from that of non-inspired scriptures.

In spite of scant information available to us about Polycarp, the available documents, of which some may have been even controversial, and yet their beliefs and stand for faith in Lord

Jesus Christ, are exemplary to us. He and others, who stood strong in faith for Lord Jesus Christ even at the cost of their lives, inspires us to hold onto the truth of the knowledge of the living God stand firm in faith to Lord Jesus Christ, the only begotten Son, who was sent into this world in order that whoever believes in Him shall not perish but have everlasting life.

IRENAEUS

Irenaeus, who was one of the early leaders in the church history, was born in Smyrna in Asia Minor. He lived from ca. 125-202, and studied under Polycarp, who was a disciple of Apostle John. Later, he became bishop of Lyons in AD 178 in Southern Gaul.

Irenaeus was very well known leader who opposed Gnosticism and his one of the works named "Against Heresies" expounded the defended the orthodox Christian beliefs. He wrote another book named "Proof of the Apostolic Preaching" in which he wrote apostles preaching about Lord Jesus Christ who fulfilled the Old Testament prophecies.

Irenaeus's eschatological views and his views on redemption of man from sin were similar to those of Apostle Paul. In the early church history Gnostic heresies played great role in deceiving Christians into paganism and undermine the deity of Lord Jesus Christ. Heretics started deification of Mary because, as they say, she bore Holy Jesus. Greek mythology had great influence on Christians who were weak in spiritual knowledge. Irenaeus held a strong view on the incarnation of God in Jesus, unity of the scriptures, and recapitulation of all things in Jesus Christ our Lord.

How the Bible Came To Us

Irenaeus believed and propagated that the first advent of Lord Jesus Christ were during the last days, that is during the end days of the world. He followed and propagated Paul's assertions in letters to Corinthians and Romans about the Adam, who was called as first Adam and Jesus, who was called the second Adam, who was also the last Adam.

What matters for us not whether these pioneers in proclaiming Gospel of Jesus Christ were bishops or whether or not Catholic Church gave them titles, such as "Saint"; but it is the right doctrines of Christ that were carried along the line from the period of ascension of Jesus to the canonization of the Bible. Their stand against heresies of Arius and Marcion are much appreciated. While heretics had questions about deity of Lord Jesus Christ, and/or treating Old Testament God bad God and the New Testament God as good God, stalwarts like Irenaeus, Athanasius, and Tertullian stood for the right doctrines.

Irenaeus had the right teaching that we all as in Adam, being sinners die, but in Christ we live, being spiritual receiving Holy Spirit. He had the right understanding about salvation within the doctrine of recapitulation. He believed and preached that the incarnate Son Lord Jesus Christ recovered that which was lost in the first Adam. Such preaching helped to show the unity of all the books in the Bible, the incarnation of God in Christ, the culmination of redemptive history in Christ Jesus, and the belief that there is salvation in Jesus alone.

References[85]:

---

[85] M.C. Steenberg. The Role of Mary as Co-recapitulator in St Irenaeus of Lyons (Vigilae Christianae, 58. 2, 2004), pp. 117-137.

How the Bible Came To Us

Irenaeus was the one who was first to say that there are only four Gospels; nothing more and nothing less. His assertion deserved acceptance because it was the truth and rightly it was an accepted fact, not only in his time period, but also later at the council of Carthage, where many other so-called gospels, like "Gospel of Mary", "Gospel of Thomas", "Shepherd of Hermas" etc., which were floating among the followers of Jesus, was rejected. What appeared as funny for some though was the reason he gave for his assertion. He said there are four zones of the universe and four winds that blow and the four wheels by the cherubims as referred to in Ezekiel 10:9.

"And when I looked, behold the four wheels by the cherubims, one wheel by one cherub, and another wheel by another cherub: and the appearance of the wheels was as the colour of a beryl stone" (Ezekiel 10:9)

Quote from Irenaeus's writing[86]:

"It is not possible that the Gospels can be either more or fewer in number than they are. For, since there are four zones of the world in which we live, and four principal winds, while the Church is scattered throughout all the world, and the "pillar and ground" of the Church is the Gospel and the spirit of life; it is fitting that she should have four pillars, breathing out immortality on every side, and vivifying men afresh. From which fact, it is evident that the Word, the Artificer of all, He that sitteth upon the cherubim, and contains all things, He who was manifested to men, has given us the Gospel under four aspects,

---

Irenaeus. Anchor Bible Dictionary. p. 458.

[86] Irenaeus of Lyons. Book III. Chapter 11 para 8 (Public Domain) n.d. web [18 June 2015]

but bound together by one Spirit. As also David says, when entreating His manifestation, "Thou that sittest between the cherubim, shine forth." For the cherubim, too, were four-faced, and their faces were images of the dispensation of the Son of God. For, [as the Scripture] says, "The first living creature was like a lion," symbolizing His effectual working, His leadership, and royal power; the second [living creature] was like a calf, signifying [His] sacrificial and sacerdotal order; but "the third had, as it were, the face as of a man,"-an evident description of His advent as a human being; "the fourth was like a flying eagle," pointing out the gift of the Spirit hovering with His wings over the Church. And therefore the Gospels are in accord with these things, among which Christ Jesus is seated"

Irenaeus, in his Book I, writes about Valentinian Gnostics tracing back up to Magician Simon Magus[87] in Acts 8:9. In Book II he writes that Valentinianism does not contain any merit in terms doctrines. In Book III he provides excerpts from Gospels and says that Valentinian doctrines are false. In Book IV he stresses on the sayings of Jesus and brings out the unity between the Old Testament and the New Testament. In Book V he not only focuses on the sayings of Jesus, but also on the sayings of Apostle Paul.

---

[87] Simon Magus was probably a Jew or a Samaritan, who had addicted himself to the arts of magic, and who was much celebrated for it. He had studied philosophy in Alexandria in Egypt, (Mosheim, i. p. 113, 114, Murdock's translation,) and then lived at Samaria. After he was cut off from the hope of adding to his other powers the power of working miracles, the Fathers say that he fell into many errors, and became the founder of the sect of the Simonians. – William Barnes Commentary

How the Bible Came To Us

TERTULLIAN

One of the early church fathers, who stood strong on the right doctrines, was Tertullian, who lived circa 150-2225 AD, but was deprived of sainthood by Roman Catholics. We really do not take into consideration whether or not he was given Sainthood by Roman Catholics, inasmuch as that matters very little for any true Christian. He took to a wrong path in his later years joining Montanism.

Very able in his presentation of theology in legal language, Tertullian wrote his views in Latin. While there were theologians writing in Greek during that period, Tertullian chose to write in Latin, which became very popular and he was officially recognized as the one who wrote Christian literature in Latin. Greek and Latin were very familiar spoken languages. Rome subsequently sanctified Latin, which became like the language of their religion.

Although his parents were from pagan origin, yet he was an excellent apologist. He was born in the city of Carthage in North Africa to one who was a centurion in Roman Government. His knowledge was of the Romans and of the Greeks, and he pursued legal career that helped him in his writings. If he did not find a suitable word to explain his view point he was not reluctant to coin a new word in Latin, and thus he contributed several new terms in the language of Latin. The most popular word that Christians use now is the word "Trinity" coined by him. Although the word is not in the bible, yet the meaning of the word is an excellent explanation of Godhead. It was accepted by evangelical Christians through the ages. The word "Trinity" denotes One God in three persons; they are not three Gods, but three in One God-head.

How the Bible Came To Us

Tertullian insistently pursued Roman Government to stop persecuting the followers of Jesus Christ. To achieve that end he wrote several books to the Romans defending Christianity. His devotion to fight against the prevalent heresies during his days was exceedingly great. Marcion movement that considered the God of Old Testament was very angry one and therefore was different from New Testament God, who was sympathetic and loving, was damaging the beliefs of Christians, who had to fight tooth and nail to emphasize that God is one and the God of the Old Testament and of the New Testament are one and the same.

In addition to the heresies of Gnostics, Tertullian also had to face tough opposition from Clement of Alexandria and Origen, who were promoting the idea that Plato's philosophy on truth deserved to be imbibed into Christian theology because, as they say, the truth is one, and there is no difference in the truth. However, Tertullian's view was that man's knowledge is antithetical to that of God, and man's knowledge is foolishness before God just God's knowledge is foolishness to the world.

During the period of Tertullian many Christians were frustrated because Jesus did not return second time, according to their time frame. The church was growing complacent with the liberal views drifting away morally steadily. It was during that time that Tertullian decided to join a sect that was following rigorous and strict rules and that was "Montanism[88]" founded

---

[88] "The Montanists believed that their founder, together with the two prophetesses Priscilla and Maximilla, were in special and direct communion with the Holy Spirit in a ministry intended to purify the Church in preparation for the coming of Jesus Christ". "Montanism". New World Encyclopedia" n.d. web [22 June 2015]. <https://creativecommons.org/licenses/by-sa/3.0/>

by Montanus. Not all the Christians considered Montanism as non-heretical.

References[89]

ATHANASIUS

Athanasius[90], who was a very prominent figure in the history of church, was born in circa 297-373 AD in the city of Alexandria of Egypt. He was a very important leader inasmuch he lived before the Nicene Council, and during and after the Nicene Council (Nicene council forms an important division in the history of Christianity). He was short dark skinned man but he was very strong in his mission and stand for Lord Jesus Christ. Undaunted by the people of his day and Constantine, emperor of his day, he fought Arian heresy successfully and emerged triumphant at the council of Nicaea.

"But the natural man receiveth not the things of the Spirit of God: for they are foolishness unto him: neither can he know them, because they are spiritually discerned" (1 Corinthians 2:14)

"For the wisdom of this world is foolishness with God. For it is written, He taketh the wise in their own craftiness" (1 Corinthians 3:19)

It is because man cannot understand God fully he tries to define God. "The wisdom of this world is foolishness with God". It took

---

[89] Benham, William (1887). The Dictionary of Religion. p. 1013.
Jerome, 'Chronicon' 16.23-4
Tertullian, De Exhortatione Castitatis 7.3 and De Monogamia 12.2

[90] Source partially depended on "Athanasius of Alexandria." New World Encyclopedia, 23 Nov 2012, 17:11 UTC. 23 Jun 2015, 08:15 <https://creativecommons.org/licenses/by-sa/3.0/>

How the Bible Came To Us

several years for man to come even close to God leave alone understanding fully as to how He is and who is. Out of ignorance many heresies also took birth. One such heresy that pestered early Christians was about the Son of God. The wicked thought propagated was that if the Father had begotten Son, the Son was not at some point of time, and the Son was a created being.

During the period of Athanasius, there was much misunderstanding about Lord Jesus Christ that He was not equal with the Father and according to Arius, who spread this heresy, very vehemently, the mention of the word "begotten" is an indication that the Son was non-existent at one point of time, and that He was begotten at a certain point, which would mean Jesus was a created being and not a God, according to Arian heresy. This heresy is active even currently among some who call themselves as Christians but are not.

God is love and Godhead exists in three persons. They concept of Trinity was understood by man much later after apostles preached the Gospel of Jesus Christ. Although there is no word namely "Trinity" in the Bible, the meaning of the word is widely accepted by Christian community. The word "Trinity" was coined by Tertullian, who was also one of the very prominent leaders in the church history.

It was very hard for Christians to get over the heresy spread by Arius and this heretical movement was catching heat of the day very forcefully. Athanasius fought tooth and nail this heresy and in doing so, he was exiled several times out of Egypt.

It was not man who defined God nor were the Scriptures written or compiled according to the wishes of some church leaders, but it is God who declared His word and revealed to His servants. Therefore, the decisions taken at the Nicene Council,

How the Bible Came To Us

and the canonization of the Bible that took place sixty years after the death of Athanasius, were according the directions and guidance of the Holy Spirit.

CHAPTER 29
CRITERIA FOR CANONIZATION

INTENT OF SCRIPTURE

"All Scripture is breathed out by God and profitable for teaching, for reproof, for correction, and for training in righteousness, that the man of God may be complete, equipped for every good work" (2 Timothy 3:16-17 ESV)

There are criteria set in every field as to who should find a place in an organization, or a school etc. Without passing an entrance examination, or an eligibility test, no one will get an admission in a Medical School, or in Engineering course, or any such important career. Filtering out the candidates in order to accommodate the best is done everywhere.

If in secular matters if such criteria are set forth, then it only goes to show to us, how seriously we need to consider as to which Scripture should be read in the Churches or by individuals, especially in view of the fact that there is no dearth of myths and false literature.

The criteria for reading the authoritative scripture by Christians is not set by the fathers of the Church but by God, who inspired them to include the Scripture that He breathed out, and reject other writings which are in the form of stories to please men of importance, and general public as a whole, in order to deviate from the Truth.

It is not the antiquity of the literature that was important to take decision but it is God's authority by His inspiration that was the criterion for the canonicity or the Bible.

How the Bible Came To Us

BARJESUS

The Scripture records of a man named "Barjesus", who was a Jew, a false prophet and a sorcerer that stood as a stumbling block in the way of a senior Government official, who held the positon of the deputy of the country named Sergius Paulus, from believing Lord Jesus Christ, who was the Way, the Truth and the Life.

Barjesus, who was known as Elymas (by the interpretation of his name), had put entire efforts to deviate from the faith Sergius Paulus, who called Barnabas and Saul (who was called Paul) desiring to hear the Word of God.

It is then that Apostle Paul set his eyes on Elymas and said "O full of all subtilty and all mischief, thou child of the devil, thou enemy of all righteousness, wilt thou not cease to pervert the right ways of the Lord? And now, behold, the hand of the Lord is upon thee, and thou shalt be blind, not seeing the sun for a season". Immediately there fell on him a mist and darkness. His obstruction did not prevent the deputy from accepting Jesus as Lord, but "when he saw what was done, believed and being astonished at the doctrine of the Lord (cf. Acts 13:6-12)

In an another occasion when a sorcerer, who was baptized, saw the people of Samaria received Holy Spirit, when Apostles Peter and John laid hands on them, he offered money to the Apostles to empower him to lay hands and invoke Holy Spirit to come upon those upon whomsoever he may lay hands. Sensing crookedness on the part of Simon, Apostle Peter said to him "Thy money perish with thee, because thou hast thought that the gift of God may be purchased with money (cf. Acts 8:18-20)

How the Bible Came To Us

In those two different cases it was seen that there were perverted people whose names are found in the Scriptures that put their entire efforts to deviate from the truth and deceive people in order that they may not exercise their faith on Lord Jesus Christ.

If people whose names are found in the Scriptures worked against the living God, then there is no wonder if secular people worked against Him. In the early days of Christianity after Lord Jesus Christ had ascended into heaven, there were many false teachings proclaimed, and many written false doctrines were circulated. Gnosticism is one such heresy that caught the air very quickly and spread among the people.

MARCION

Perhaps, the necessity for New Testament Canon and the urgency occurred because of the serious and severe departure from the Truth, resulting in spreading of false literature by Gnostics, whose prime leader, as some suppose is one named Marcion[91].

Marcion[92] was an influential rich man, who owned a shipping company, which was the chief port of Pontus, at Sinope, in Turkey, on the southern shore of the Black Sea. He, who was a bishop, was also a bishop.

Marcion's theology refuted "Jehovah", as seen in the Old Testament, on reasons that He was unapproachable, harsh, and unmerciful. By the end of 144 AD clergy of Christians in Rome discussed about his theology and saw that he was on purpose

---

[91] Tertull. I. 6: "Marcion non negat creatorem deum esse."
[92] "History of Dogma - Volume I" Ch.5:1, Christian Classics Ethereal Library n.d. web[04 June 2015]

How the Bible Came To Us

propagating monstrous doctrines that became huge threat to the Christendom. He was quickly excommunicated and his generous contributions made to the church were returned.

TEST THE SPIRITS

Scripture proves scripture and scriptures cannot be broken. Lord Jesus referred to Old Testament Scriptures several times and held Sadducees, Pharisees and Scribes held responsible and accountable for the knowledge in Scriptures.

If the Scriptures were not true how a Godly Jew would have considered the Book of Isaiah or Jeremiah or Chronicles as Scriptures. The Scriptures are God-breathed and not those that were written by a prophet purportedly revealed to him by God. If a palm is held against the mouth and man breathes out certain amount of pressure is felt; similar is the case of God-breathing out His words that became Scripture. God is not a creature but a Spirit, who cannot be seen by man's physical eyes. He spoke to man in different ways in different dispensations. When he spoke to Prophets, they said "Thus says the Lord[93]", and when the Scripture from the Old Testament is quoted the phrase used is "it is written[94]". Anyone who despises John 1:1, and John 1:14 does not belong to God[95].

---

[93] Example: Thus saith the LORD, Ye shall not go up, nor fight against your brethren the children of Israel: return every man to his house; for this thing is from me. They hearkened therefore to the word of the LORD, and returned to depart, according to the word of the LORD. (1 Kings 12:24); Also cf. 1 Chronicles 17:3–4; Jeremiah 35:13; Ezek. 2:4; Zech. 7:9; etc.

[94] Notes: Cf. Jos 8:31; 2Sa 1:18; 1Ki 2:3; 2Ki 23:21; 2Ch 23:18; 25:4; 31:3; 35:12; Ezr. 3:2,4; 6:18; Ne 6:6; 8:15; 10:34,36; Es 1:19; 8:8-9; Ps 40:7; Isa 4:3; 65:6; Jer 17:1; 25:13; Da 9:13; Mt 2:5; 4:4,6-7,10; 11:10; 21:13; 26:24,31; Mr. 1:2; 7:6; 9:12-13; 11:17; 14:21,27; Lu 2:23; 3:4; 4:4,8,10; 7:27; 19:46; 24:46; Joh 6:31,45; 8:17; 10:34; 12:14; Ac 1:20; 7:42; 13:33; 15:15; 23:5; Ro 1:17; 2:24; 3:4,10; 4:17; 8:36; 9:13,33; 10:15; 11:8,26; 12:19; 14:11; 15:3,9,21; 1Co 1:19,31; 2:9; 3:19; 9:9-10; 10:7; 14:21; 15:45; 2Co 4:13; 8:15; 9:9; Ga 3:10,13;

How the Bible Came To Us

"In the beginning was the Word, and the Word was with God, and the Word was God" (John 1:1)

"And the Word was made flesh, and dwelt among us, (and we beheld his glory, the glory as of the only begotten of the Father,) full of grace and truth" (John 1:14)

The authority of the Scriptures was confirmed and ratified by Lord Jesus Christ.

"Hereby know ye the Spirit of God: Every spirit that confesseth that Jesus Christ is come in the flesh is of God" (1 John 4:2)

Lord Jesus did not leave behind any writing but His teachings were made available in writing by his disciples, the chief among who was Apostle Paul. His argument is noteworthy.

"Do we begin again to commend ourselves? or need we, as some others, epistles of commendation to you, or letters of commendation from you? Ye are our epistle written in our hearts, known and read of all men: Forasmuch as ye are manifestly declared to be the epistle of Christ ministered by us, written not with ink, but with the Spirit of the living God; not in tables of stone, but in fleshy tables of the heart" (2 Corinthians 3:1-3)

SCRIPTURE

Paul' letters were authentic scriptures that have been acknowledged as Scripture not only by the churches to which he sent them out but by the Church as a whole. The Book of

---

4:22,27; Heb. 10:7; 1Pe 1:16; 1Jo 2:21
[95] cf. 1 Cor. 16:21; Gal. 6:11; Col. 4:18; 2 Thess. 3: 17; also Philemon 19

How the Bible Came To Us

Hebrews[96] is accepted as the work of Paul by the church of Alexandria and as canonical.

The Holy Bible claims that Jesus Christ is God (cf. Isaiah 9:6-7; Matthew 1:22-23; John 1:1,2,14; 20:28; Acts 16:31, 34; Philippians 2:5-6; Colossians 2:9; Titus 2:13; Hebrews 1:8; 2 Peter 1:1) and yet secular literature that claim to be scripture does not the claim of the Bible as true. When such contradiction surfaces the Bible is to be trusted; it is the Word of God.

Apostle Paul's writing has a definite and interesting clue to the Scripture that was inspired by God. He called Timothy, who accompanied him in his missionary journeys, as his son. Paul and Silas travel from Troas to Samothracia, Neapolis, and Philippi preaching the Gospel, and call for Timothy, who was at Troas to come with cloak that he left with Carpus at Troas and "also the books and above all the parchments (writing base made of animal skins, on which the ancient books were written). Much later in the history after Apostle Paul's death these writings, either of his own or of others, were, obviously included in the canonical Bible.

It is, therefore, evident that the books that were included while canonization, were not included by choice of the church fathers, but by the veracity of God's out-breathed content, and the availability of supporting scriptures in other books.

It is not because the books were in the Bible that they became the Scripture, but because they were God-breathed Scriptures that they found their way into the Canon. It is not because the church fathers included the books in the Bible that the books

---

[96] F.F. Bruce. The Canon of Scripture. Downers Grove, IVP, 1988, Chapter 21.

How the Bible Came To Us

became inspired books, but because God guided the church fathers to include His out-breathed Word the books were included in the Bible.

"When you come, bring the cloak that I left with Carpus at Troas, also the books, and above all the parchments" (2 Timothy 4:13 ESV)

There is a very definite pointing to the inspired scriptures in the Old Testament where Daniel makes a reference, from the letter from Jeremiah, of the prophecy of seventy-year captivity and their release thereafter.

"in the first year of his reign, I, Daniel, perceived in the books the number of years that, according to the word of the LORD to Jeremiah the prophet, must pass before the end of the desolations of Jerusalem, namely, seventy years" (Daniel 9:2 ESV)

"For thus saith the LORD, That after seventy years be accomplished at Babylon I will visit you, and perform my good word toward you, in causing you to return to this place". (Jeremiah 29:10)

"To fulfil the word of the LORD by the mouth of Jeremiah, until the land had enjoyed her sabbaths: for as long as she lay desolate she kept sabbath, to fulfil threescore and ten years" (2 Chronicles 36:21; also cf. Jeremiah 30:18; Jeremiah 31:38)

Some of the important criteria set forth for recognition of New Testament books were whether or not

- The author was an apostle or worked with an apostle
- The book was accepted by the Church (the body of Christ) in general

How the Bible Came To Us

- The writings contain consistent doctrine and orthodox beliefs
- The writings depict high moral and spiritual values that reflect Holy Spirit's guidance and conviction

Thus, in canonizing the Bible with the Scriptures that met the above criteria, spurious and deceitful books containing myths, and those that were written to please some vested interests, were rejected

CHAPTER 30
ROLE OF CONSTANTINE

Flavius V Aurelius Constantine commonly known as Constantine I was a Roman Emperor (274 AD to 337 AD), who worshipped Pagan gods, especially sun god, Sol. However, when he was confronted by Maxentius, a very powerful rival from Italy, he saw vision wherein he saw a cross of Jesus Christ superimposed on the sun with words "in hoc signo vinces", which meant "in this sign you shall conquer". The vision came true and he won the battle. It was from that time onward that he became a great devotee of Jesus Christ.

Until fourth century no one celebrated Christmas, the birth of Jesus, but on Constantine's initiative two festivals were celebrated in the month of December according to Roman calendar from AD 336. Both these festivals were intended to honor pagan gods, one of which was Saturn, the Roman god of agriculture and another was celebrated in commemoration of the birth of Mithras, the Persian god of light. The first one lasted for seven days from December 17th and the second one from December 25 lasting through January 1.

These two festivals were merged into one and one single festival called "Christmas" was celebrated. Thus was born the story of Christmas and continued until this day to celebrate Christ's undefined birth date and gifts are exchanged and parties conducted among families and friends.

Rome, during his period, did not have Bible as a religious sacred scripture for people to read in the churches and in homes but they had script on scrolls to read from. Also there was a boiling question prevalent during those days as to whether Jesus was God or man or both.

In order to maintain unity of people in his country and to have for himself scriptures in the form of book, he convened a council at Nicaea in 325 AD.

THE COUNCIL OF NICAEA

Constantine's desire was never to establish, on his own, or through the council, the doctrine of divinity of Lord Jesus Christ. Neither he nor the council had authority to define God as God and whether or not Lord Jesus was God or man or both.

The scriptures are clear that Lord Jesus Christ is God and He descended into this earth in the form of servant and in the likeness of man and dwelt among us. The Word became flesh and He lived among us. The Lord's purpose, ultimately, to become propitiation for us in order that by confessing Him as the Lord and by believing that God raised Him from the dead we would become children of God.

Therefore, it is evident that before any man could define who He was, His divinity and His incarnation was known several hundred years before Constantine convened the council at Nicaea. Constantine was a man and not someone above God to define God. His intention was only to bring unification in the country in order that he may have peaceful reign.

People during the life of Jesus on earth thought that Jesus was a prophet but their thinking changed after Lord Jesus rose from the dead and appeared to many. The deity of Jesus was known from then onward. Some unknowingly accuse that it was

How the Bible Came To Us

Constantine who was the reason to establish the deity of Jesus at the Council of Nicaea[97].

In fact, the council of Nicaea did not debate whether or not Jesus was the "Son of God", nor did Constantine control the council. His aim was to retain peace in his country and he did that which he wrought to do. He, being a man, and nothing more, could not make a man God nor could he make any God into man.

Constantine neither had any part in forming the Bible or canonization of the Bible but he had a role to convene the Nicene Council, which was the first Christian Church General Conference under his regime. It was convened to take a decision s about the canonization of the Bible, which came into fruition after in 397 AD of the council that met in 325 AD. Constantine lived from 274 AD to 337 AD and he had become emperor of Rome in 306 AD and Bible was canonized sixty years after his death. Twenty one books of the Bible were already accepted By Christians.

Christians were in total dilemma as to which books they were to read and what form of worship was the right one. There was no dearth of Christian literature written by individual writers circulating. Along with this came the confusion brought in by one Bishop named Arius, who said Jesus was not a God, but he was a highest form of created man. This heresy was too much for Christians to assimilate into their beliefs, and then came up another bishop named Athnasius from Alexandria who opposed very strongly Arian heresy and stood up boldly to proclaim that Jesus is both man and God.

---

[97] "The Council of Nicaea". All About God Ministries, n.d. Web[12 June. 2015]

How the Bible Came To Us

Caught in the middle of these arguments was Constantine who feared disintegration of his kingdom, and therefore, called for a meeting of all the bishops from Rome to participate and knock down to a uniform belief that would be acceptable to everyone and would bring unity in his kingdom.

Eusebius, a Bishop from Caesarea found collection of manuscripts from the Libraries at Jerusalem and Caesarea and compiled a collection of eighteen books.

There was a declaration made in the Nicene council after close and intense deliberations that Jesus was both man and God. They all agreed that the right interpretation of Scriptures is that Jesus had two natures; one of God and another of man. He was both divine and human. That is how Nicene Creed was formed. It reads...

How the Bible Came To Us

The Book of Common Prayer Episcopal [98]

We believe in one God,
the Father, the Almighty,
maker of heaven and earth,
of all that is, seen and unseen.

We believe in one Lord, Jesus Christ,
the only Son of God,
eternally begotten of the Father,
God from God, Light from Light,
true God from true God,
begotten, not made,
of one Being with the Father.
Through him all things were made.
For us and for our salvation
he came down from heaven:
by the power of the Holy Spirit
he became incarnate from the Virgin Mary,
and was made man.
For our sake he was crucified under Pontius Pilate;
he suffered death and was buried.
On the third day he rose again
in accordance with the Scriptures;
he ascended into heaven
and is seated at the right hand of the Father.
He will come again in glory to judge the living and the dead,
and his kingdom will have no end.

We believe in the Holy Spirit, the Lord, the giver of life,
who proceeds from the Father and the Son.

---

[98] (Nicene Creed. Public Domain. 325 AD) Creeds of Christendom, n.d. web [12 June, 2015]

How the Bible Came To Us

With the Father and the Son he is worshiped and glorified.
He has spoken through the Prophets.
We believe in one holy catholic and apostolic Church.
We acknowledge one baptism for the forgiveness of sins.
We look for the resurrection of the dead,
and the life of the world to come. Amen.

How the Bible Came To Us

NICENE CREED
Nicene Creed Papyrus

Image © The John Rylands Library_Manchester_UK

Nicene creed
Author: Council of Nicea
Public Domain {{{PD-1923}}}
Source: http://enriqueta.man.ac.uk/luna/servlet/s/4pq780
This file has been identified as being free of known restrictions under copyright law, including all related and neighboring rights.
https://creativecommons.org/publicdomain/mark/1.0/deed.en

Constantine ordered in AD 330 fifty copies of the Bible in full for his own use and financed the project. The copies of the Bibles that were presented to him had in them, the 21 New Testament

How the Bible Came To Us

Books that Christians already preached and studied from. Those books were four Gospels, Acts of the Apostles, and Paul's letters. The disputed books that were subject to debate and they were II and III John, II Peter, James, Jude, Apocalypse of John (Revelation)

Sixty years after the death of Constantine i.e. in AD 397 the Bible was canonized[99].

The first canon was "Muratorian Canon". It was a fragment containing a list of Scriptural canonical books compiled in Greek. Latin manuscript, which was found by Cardinal L.A. Muratory (1672-1750) in "Ambrosian Library" in Milan Italy, had the principles, which were to be followed to recognize the books in the Bible, were written in AD 170. The document refers to the office of Pope Pius who died in 157It was the only Scriptural book the date of which can be traced to 2nd Century and, therefore, Scholars assign its date as from 4th Century. Except for Hebrews, James, and 3rd John it had all other New Testament books.

At the council of Laodicea, in AD 363, it was decided that the Old Testament along with Apocrypha books and the New Testament with 27 books should be read in the Churches.

At the Council of Hippo, in AD 393 and at the Council of Carthage, in AD 397 it was reiterated that the Old Testament with Apocrypha books and 27 New Testament Books should be read. This decision was the authoritative instruction for the canon of the Bible[100],[101].

---

[99] NPNF2-04. Athanasius: Select Works and Letters. Christian Classics Ethereal Library n.d. web[12 June 2015]
[100] Pavao, Paul. "The Muratorian Canon", Christian History for Everyman.

How the Bible Came To Us

Symbolum Nicaenum A.D. 325   [Public Domain]

Πιστεύομεν εις ένα Θεον Πατερα παντοκράτορα, πάντων ορατων τε και αοράτων ποιητήν.

Πιστεύομεν εισ ένα κύριον Ἰησουν Χριστον, τον υἰον του θεου, γεννηζέντα εκ του πατρος μονογενη, τουτέστιν εκ της ουσίας του πατρός, θεον εκ θεου αληθινου, γεννηθέντα, ου ποιηθέντα, ὁμοούσιον τωι πατρί δι οὖ τα πάντα εγένετο, τα τε εν τωι ουρανωι και τα επι της γης τον δι ἡμας τους ανθρώπους και δα την ἡμετέραν σωτηρίαν κατελθόντα και σαρκωθέντα και ενανθρωπήσαντα, παθόντα, και αναστάντα τηι τριτηι ἡμέραι, και ανελθοντα εις τους οθρανούς, και ερχόμενον κριναι ζωντασ και νεκρούς.

Και εις το Ἁγιον Πνευμα.
Τους δε λέγοντας, ὁτι ἡν ποτε ὁτε οθκ ἡν, και πριν γεννηθηναι ουκ ἡν, και ὁτι εξ ἑτερας ὑποστάσεως η ουσιας φάσκοντας ειναι, [η κτιστόν,] τρεπτον η αλλοιωτον τον υἰον του θεου, [τούτους] αναθεματίζει ἡ καθολικη [και αποστολικη] εκκλησία.

"Symbolum Nicaenum A.D. 325" Creeds of Christendom. n.d. web[12 June 2015]

Greatest Stories Ever Told. 2014. Web[13 June 2015].
[101] "How and when was the canon of the Bible put together?" Got Questions Ministries, n.d. Web. [12 June 2015]

CHAPTER 31
THREE THOUSAND YEARS IN NUTSHELL

Leslie M. John

FIRST WRITTEN WORD

Moses was born in about 1500 BC and he spent forty years in Pharaoh's residence, and forty years in Midian and then led Israel for forty years in the wilderness. God gave the children of Israel the Ten Commandments by the hand of Moses in about 1420 BC. It was the first written Word of God. It was not until 500 BC the script developed and thirty nine book of the Hebrew Bible was made into codex. Thereafter, in about 500 BC the Hebrew Bible was translated by seventy scholars into Greek and the codex thus made was called "Septuagint".

THE SEPTUAGINT

The Septuagint contained not only 39 Books of the Hebrew Bible, which we call as the "Old Testament" but also the text of 15 Apocrypha books scattered in the codex at various places. The Apocrypha books had relevance only for historical purposes, and although they were included in 1611 KJB they were subsequently removed.

THE NEW TESTAMENT

After the ascension of Lord Jesus Christ, apostles proclaimed the Gospel of Jesus Christ and by the end of 1st Century the original Greek manuscripts containing the details of the life of Jesus, and few letters of apostles, and apocalypse (the Revelation) total 27 books were made up into one book called the "New Testament"

COUNCIL OF NICAEA

At the Council of Nicaea some important decisions were taken and sixty years after the death of Athanasius, the Bishop of Alexandria the Bible was canonized with 39 Old Testament Books, 27 Old Testament Books and 15 Apocrypha Books in 397 AD. Jerome translated the Greek Bible into Latin and it was the "vulgate" in the fourth century probably in 382 AD. Thereafter, the Bible was translated into several languages.

JOHN WYCLIFFE BIBLE

As far as English Bible is concerned John Wycliffe was the first one who translated the Bible into English Language in 1384 AD. He lived from 1330-1384 and spoke boldly against the corruptions in the church and some of its depraved unscriptural doctrines. His 1000-page book "The Truth of Scripture" speaks all about the value and the authority of the inspired Scriptures.

MARTIN LUTHER'S BIBLE

Martin Luther translated New Testament in 1522 AD and the Old Testament in 1534 AD. He lived form 1483-1546 AD and spent much of his life in sin; however he found relief in the forgiveness of sin by Lord Jesus Christ by accepting Him as Savior. The Gospel of Jesus Christ weighed greatly in his work for the Lord and while pondering over scriptures deeply he found that man cannot achieve righteousness by his own works but the salvation is free gift from God. It is then that he decided that German people should have the privilege of reading the Bible in their own language.

How the Bible Came To Us

PRINTING PRESS

Printing Press was invented in 1455 AD by Johannes Gutenberg, a German, and the first book in print media was the Gutenberg's Bible in Latin.

ERASMUS BIBLE

In 1516 AD Desiderius Erasmus produced Greek/Latin Parallel New Testament. Erasmus lived from 1496-1536 AD. He opposed the conspiracy of the church in prohibiting the translations of the Bible into various languages. The church ventured to maintain control over people forever; but alas! Bold men like Erasmus stood firmly against such attitude. He not only wished that the scriptures be made available to not only to Scots and Irish, but also to Turks and Saracens. He propagated the view the women should be given the privilege of reading the Gospels and letters of apostles. Six Greek manuscripts were made use of by Erasmus and thus his work was unique when he produced Greek New Testament; notwithstanding it fell short of expectations inasmuch as the older manuscripts such as Uncials and Greek Papyri were not depended on. However, his work was helpful in subsequent editions.

WILLIAM TYNDALE BIBLE

The first New Testament in print media in English was by William Tyndale in 1526 AD. Tyndale spoke against the corruptions in the church, neither sparing clergy nor laity, just as one of his predecessors John Wycliffe did. He based his translation of the Bible on the Greek New Testament that was published by Erasmus.

How the Bible Came To Us

THE GREAT BIBLE

The first authorized Bible for public use in print media in English language was the "Great Bible" in 1539 AD. Tyndale was persecuted when one of his friends, whom he befriended, betrayed him. Tyndale was imprisoned for five hundred days before he was burned to death at the stake in 1536. Tyndale prayed while leaving his spirit saying "Oh Lord, open the King of England's eyes" and the Lord God answered his prayer, when in1539, just three years after his prayer was offered. King Henry VIII not only conceded to the request of printing English Bible but funded the project and the result was the production of "Great Bible".

MYLES COVERDALE BIBLE

The first complete Bible known as "Myles Coverdale's Bible" in print media in English, which had Old Testament, New Testament and Apocrypha Books, came out in 1535 AD. While there was a flurry of productions of English Bibles during the reign of Henry VIII (1509-1547), even though he did not take initiative in such venture, Tyndale's colleague named Miles Coverdale completed a translation of the Bible that made inroads into land of British. Another colleague of Tyndale named John Rogers who opted to be called by his nick name "Thomas Matthew" also completed translation of English Bible in 1537 AD and it received Royal sanction. Thus the second complete Bible in print media in English was the "Tyndale-Matthews Bible" done by John "Thomas Matthew" in 1537 AD

GENEVA BIBLE

The "Geneva Bible" was very popular in 16th Century. The Geneva Bible was almost similar to the present day King James

How the Bible Came To Us

Bible, but many did not perceive it that way inasmuch as new editions, and new versions, and new translations emerged.

The complete version of the Geneva Bible was first published in 1560 AD and before that the New Testament was published in 1557 AD. Geneva Bible was refuted as "Breeches Bible" by some based on a passage from Genesis, where the skin clothing God provided for Adam and Eve, was termed in the Geneva Bible as "Breeches[102]". The word was an antiquated form of "Britches[103]". (Breeches are knee-length trousers often having ornamental buckles, while the word "britches" is a noun used with plural verb).

The Geneva Bible was the first one to use the numbering of the verses to the chapters in the Bible. The provision of marginal references helped to study the Bible with ease, and therefore, it was called the first English "Study Bible". These references from the Geneva Bible that helped like a good concordance were extensively used by Shakespeare in his plays. With the publication of 144 editions of the Geneva Bible between 1560 AD and 1644 AD greatly helped 1611 King James Bible translators. With the popularity 1611 King James Bible and other versions gained the Geneva Bible was almost shelved from 1644 AD.

1611 AUTHORIZED VERSION (KING JAMES BIBLE)

In 1611 AD the authorized version of the Bible (also called the King James Bible) was printed with 39 Old Testament Books, 27

---

[102] "breeches." *Online Etymology Dictionary*. Douglas Harper, Historian. 25 Jun. 2015.
[103] "britches." *Dictionary.com Unabridged*. Random House, Inc. 25 Jun. 2015.

How the Bible Came To Us

New Testament books and 15 Apocrypha Books, which were placed after the Old Testament and before the New Testament. However, 15 Apocrypha books were removed from the Bibles that Protestants use.

Thereafter the Bible was translated into several languages and several revisions made to suite to the spoken languages of the people all over the world. Source depended on[104]

---

[104] English Bible History. "greatsite.com" n.d. web[24 June 2015] <WWW.GREATSITE.COM>

How the Bible Came To Us

SECTION II
SALVATION MESSAGES

CHAPTER 32
SAVED BY GRACE

"Now therefore why tempt ye God, to put a yoke upon the neck of the disciples, which neither our fathers nor we were able to bear?" (Acts 15:10)

Apostle Peter rose up in the council at Jerusalem to ask a question as to why a great burden was being laid on men to believe God that certain rituals need to be observed to receive salvation. This situation occurred when some obstructionists entered into Christianity and said mere faith in Jesus was not enough to be saved but circumcision was necessary.

It was a time in the first century AD when Gospel of Jesus Christ was being proclaimed with great vigor, first in Jerusalem, and then in Judea and Samaria, and then in the uttermost parts of the world.

There were stringent laws and the obligations laid down in the Old Testament for offering sacrifices and oblations in order for one's sins to be covered. There was no remission of sins, but only covering of the sins, during the Old Testament period.

God was so unapproachable that it was only High Priest, who went into the "Holy of Holies" in the Tabernacle, once a year, and he alone could intercede with the LORD on behalf of people. It was at the "Mercy Seat" that God spoke to Moses and Aaron.

The High priest sprinkled the blood of the sacrificed animal, on behalf of the entire congregation, upon the "Mercy Seat", and it was accepted by the LORD as an atonement of sins of the

How the Bible Came To Us

people. The high priest went out and confessed the sins upon the 'scapegoat' which was, then sent out into the wilderness, never to return again. This provided temporary covering of the sins of the people but not remission of sins altogether.

There was a time period to complete, and after all these things were done, God sent His only Son, in due time, into this world to become propitiation for us. The Father, and the Son, and the Holy Spirit are one God in Trinity; and they are not three Gods. Lord Jesus Christ relinquished His glory with the Father and incarnated as man to bear the sin of mankind, and provide a perfect sacrifice. He became sacrifice on behalf of us and provided way to obtain salvation. The sacrifices offered in the Old Testament period, were the shadows of the things that were to be fulfilled in Lord Jesus Christ.

"But when the fulness of the time was come, God sent forth his Son, made of a woman, made under the law" (Galatians 4:4)

There is no remission of sins unless blood was shed and that demand is fulfilled by Lord Jesus Christ on behalf of us, bearing our shame, our iniquity, and our sin upon Him, and becoming sin for our sake. He was without sin. He was holy and had no blemish in His life. He bore our sin on behalf of us, in order that we may be saved by confessing our sins to Him, and acknowledge with mouth that He is the Lord, and believe in heart that God raised Him from the dead.

There are no strings attached to it, and we do not need to do any additional good work to receive salvation. He paid it all by His precious blood. It is not by silver or gold, or by visiting any holy shrine that we receive salvation but by accepting the fact that Jesus died and rose again on behalf of us. Good works follow the salvation; they do not precede salvation. No one can be saved by doing good works. It is all by grace through faith that we receive salvation and everlasting life.

"Forasmuch as ye know that ye were not redeemed with corruptible things, as silver and gold, from your vain conversation received by tradition from your fathers; But with the precious blood of Christ, as of a lamb without blemish and without spot" (1 Peter 1:18-19)

CHAPTER 33
GOD LIVES IN OUR HEARTS

The king said to Nathan the prophet, "See now, I dwell in a house of cedar, but the ark of God dwells in a tent." (2 Samuel 7:2 ESV))

King David, who had an ardent desire to build a house for the God, said to Nathan the prophet that it is not proper for the Ark of God to be behind curtains while he lived in a posh house made of Cedar wood. The prophet extemporaneously said to David that he may do according to his heart's desire, but when God said to the prophet and question him if he is capable of build a house for God to dwell in.

Cedar wood is incorruptible. Houses made of wooden were considered as posh living Houses in the Old Testament period, more so, if they were made of Cedar wood. King David lived in one such house made of Cedar wood (Cf.2 Samuel 5:11).

As God desired the prophet went to the king and asked him if he is capable of building the house for God. The LORD reminded David through Nathan the prophet that He never asked any of the tribes of the children of Israel while they were on their journey from Egypt to Canaan to build a house for Him except to set up a temporary portable tent called the "Tabernacle" wherever they went.

The LORD said to David by the word of the mouth of the prophet to recollect his status as a shepherd boy from where he was lifted to occupy the highest position as the King of Israel. It was God who made him not only a King over Israel but He cut out of his sight all his enemies and made his name greater than any king upon this earth.

God saw the affliction of the children of Israel, who served Pharaoh of Egypt as slaves, and brought them out of the bondage of slavery into a land flowing with milk and honey and promised to give them the to possess it. He assured them that if they served the LORD with fervor none would be able to afflict them anymore.

After they had come into the Promised Land, it was first theocracy, when God ruled them by the judges, but they wanted a king to rule over them. God hesitatingly made Saul as king over them, but because he did not obey the LORD fully, the LORD removed him from kingship and made David as the King over Israel.

God caused David to rest from all his enemies and said that the LORD will build a house for him and when his days on this earth are fulfilled he will make him sleep with his fathers. The LORD also promised that David's son Solomon will sit on his throne, and his Kingdom will be established forever, provided Solomon kept the commandments and statutes of the LORD. He also said that it is because David was a man of war, and his hands are full with blood, Solomon will build a house for the LORD.

God said that if Solomon committed any iniquity he would chastise him with rod of men, and with the stripes of the children of men, but His mercy will not depart from him.

King David humbled himself after hearing God's word through Nathan the prophet and exalted the name of God by saying:

How the Bible Came To Us

"Wherefore thou art great, O LORD God: for there is none like thee, neither is there any God beside thee, according to all that we have heard with our ears" (2 Samuel 7:22)

"And let thy name be magnified for ever, saying, The LORD of hosts is the God over Israel: and let the house of thy servant David be established before thee" (2 Samuel 7:26)

Solomon built a temple for the LORD and quickly realizes that God is so big that heaven of heavens cannot contain Him.

Isaiah 66:1 reads...

"Thus saith the LORD, The heaven is my throne, and the earth is my footstool: where is the house that ye build unto me? and where is the place of my rest?"

Solomon said:

"But will God indeed dwell with man on the earth? Behold, heaven and the highest heaven cannot contain you, how much less this house that I have built! (2 Chronicles 6:18 ESV)

Apostle Paul says God lives in our hearts.

"Know ye not that ye are the temple of God, and that the Spirit of God dwelleth in you?" (1 Corinthians 3:16)

"Know ye not that your bodies are the members of Christ? shall I then take the members of Christ, and make them the members of an harlot? God forbid. What? know ye not that he which is joined to an harlot is one body? for two, saith he, shall be one flesh" (1 Corinthians 6:15-16)

CHAPTER 34
PETER AND JOHN TESTIFY

"While he yet spake, behold, a bright cloud overshadowed them: and behold a voice out of the cloud, which said, This is my beloved Son, in whom I am well pleased; hear ye him" (Matthew 17:5)

Peter and the two sons of Zebedee (James and John), who saw Lord Jesus when He had transfiguration, testified to the world that the face of Lord Jesus Christ was like that of the Sun, and His raiment like that of white light.

In the early days of Christianity, i.e., after the ascension of Lord Jesus Christ into heaven, many false stories circulated about Jesus to cause people to develop unbelief in Him. Peter, the disciple of Jesus, was perturbed on hearing false stories, and therefore, he along with James and John, bore witness to the world, of the Lord's transfiguration. They bore witness of what they saw of His glory on the holy mountain and also heard the voice from heaven saying, "...This is my beloved Son, in whom I am well pleased; hear ye him..." (Matthew 17:5; 2 Peter 1:16-18).

Peter and other disciples did not follow cunning fables devised to deceive people, but they were physical witnesses to the live events of the ministry of Lord Jesus Christ's ministry. They testified to the audience that they were present at the very scene where the Lord transfigured to show His Majesty and glory to them.

How the Bible Came To Us

Peter heard Lord Jesus say that the Father loves His Son and that the Son has the power to lay down His life and take it again. (John 10:17).

John testified that "the Word was made flesh, and dwelt among us, (and we beheld his glory, the glory as of the only begotten of the Father,) full of grace and truth". (John 1:14)

True, we enjoy the benefits of the love of God because Jesus laid down his life our sake; "But God raised him from the dead" (Acts 13:30). We are cleansed of our sins by the blood of Jesus Christ shed on the cross. This is the truth and faith in him alone saves a person from damnation.

There was much distortion of the truth in the early days of Christianity deliberately by some who followed Gnosticism, which deals with self-realization. Peter mentions in 1 Peter 2:1-2 about false teachings prevalent during his ministry.

"But there were false prophets also among the people, even as there shall be false teachers among you, who privily shall bring in damnable heresies, even denying the Lord that bought them, and bring upon themselves swift destruction. And many shall follow their pernicious ways; by reason of whom the way of truth shall be evil spoken of" (2 Peter 2:1-2)

Gnosticism teaches that man can unite with God by understanding fully what he is and realizing who he is and gaining spiritual knowledge is the road to salvation. It does not teach salvation by grace through faith nor does it believe in Church or sacraments. Gnostics believe that a lower level of god created the universe and men are held captive devoid of special knowledge, which, according to them, is 'gnosis.

How the Bible Came To Us

Gnostics believe that abstinence from material wealth, and material world would bring them self-realization and of the many restrictions it included dietary restrictions, circumcision, avoiding commandments against adultery and fornication. It means adultery and fornication were not sins in their view. According to them Lord Jesus was a spiritual being, who came from spiritual world, and had a spiritual body and did not have a physical body on His resurrection. This was an unbearable heresy for Christians.

The Holy Bible says...

"For many deceivers are entered into the world, who confess not that Jesus Christ is come in the flesh. This is a deceiver and an antichrist" (2 John 1:7)

"For there are certain men crept in unawares, who were before of old ordained to this condemnation, ungodly men, turning the grace of our God into lasciviousness, and denying the only Lord God, and our Lord Jesus Christ" (Jude 1:4)

Do not trust every spirit, but test the sprits to know for yourself whether or not those spirits are of God. There are many false prophets and preachers gone out into this world. The way to know whether someone is from the living God or not, is to make sure whether or not that person confesses the incarnation of Lord Jesus Christ and lived among us. Anyone, who does not confess that Jesus is come in the flesh, is not of God but of antichrist. There are many out there now who say that a man can gain salvation by good works. It is time we know them and realize that they are not from God.

If you are not yet saved, here is word from Apostle Paul, who says that if you confess with your mouth the Lord Jesus and

How the Bible Came To Us

believe in your heart that God raised him from the dead you shall be saved. (Romans 10:9)

CHAPTER 35
UNLESS YOU BELIEVE

"He said to them, "You are from below; I am from above. You are of this world; I am not of this world. I told you that you would die in your sins, for unless you believe that I am he you will die in your sins." (John 8:23-24 ESV)

Lord Jesus Christ humbled Himself and came down from heaven, leaving behind His glory with the Father, and not taking pride that He was equal with the Father. He came in the form of a servant and in the likeness of man to live among us. He preached salvation message and died on the cross as a perfect sacrifice on behalf of us. In order that we may be relieved of bearing our sin, He bore our sins upon Himself on behalf us, and after His death on the cross He was buried, and God raised Him from the dead.

There is no one on the earth who could lay down His life on His own volition and take it up again, but there was one and only one who said that He had the power to lay down His life and take it up again (cf. John 10:17-18). He died on behalf us, becoming sin for our sake, in order that we may receive salvation. After dying like a poor man He was buried in rich man's tom, in fulfillment of the prophecies and was raised from the dead.

"For this reason the Father loves me, because I lay down my life that I may take it up again. No one takes it from me, but I lay it down of my own accord. I have authority to lay it down, and I have authority to take it up again. This charge I have received from my Father." (John 10:17-18 ESV)

How the Bible Came To Us

On the first day of the week, as Mary Magdalene and other Mary went to the tomb to see the sepulcher, there was a great earthquake, and the angel of the Lord came down from heaven and rolled back the stone from the door

When Mary Magdalene and other Mary went to see the tomb they found the tomb empty. The stone was rolled away. Lord Jesus broke the seal of Roman Government that was upon the tombstone, and came out from the grave; and while He was in the grave His body did not see corruption. Two men who stood by them in shining garments said to them that Lord Jesus rose from the dead and questioned them as to why they were seeking the living among the dead (cf. Luke 24:1-10).

It is so clear from the Scriptures and Historical evidences that He appeared to many for forty days after His resurrection and then ascended into heaven. As the disciples of Jesus and others watched His ascension the two men standing there said to them that Jesus will return in the same manner as He ascended into heaven.

"And while they were gazing into heaven as he went, behold, two men stood by them in white robes, and said, "Men of Galilee, why do you stand looking into heaven? This Jesus, who was taken up from you into heaven, will come in the same way as you saw him go into heaven." (Acts 1:10-11 ESV)

Bible says everyone is a born-sinner, and it is determined that the death being the wages of sin, everyone will die, but the gift of God is eternal life. Lord Jesus, who was divine and human as well, died substitutionary death on behalf of us and therefore, we all have the provision of being raised from the dead, provided we confess with our mouth that Jesus is Lord and God raised Him from the dead.

How the Bible Came To Us

This is the salvation message and anyone who believes it as true can receive it or reject it and reap the consequence, which is eternal punishment in the 'lake of fire'. The "lake of fire" is a place where there is forever, gnashing of teeth and thirst that does not quench, neither would the fire get extinguished.

When Lord Jesus was on this earth He told the truth about everlasting life through Him and about eternal death, which in Revelation is described as second death.

"Blessed and holy is he that hath part in the first resurrection: on such the second death hath no power, but they shall be priests of God and of Christ, and shall reign with him a thousand years" (Revelation 20:6)

"But the fearful, and unbelieving, and the abominable, and murderers, and whoremongers, and sorcerers, and idolaters, and all liars, shall have their part in the lake which burneth with fire and brimstone: which is the second death" (Revelation 21:8)

Pharisees, Scribes and Sadducees were always in confrontation with Lord Jesus Christ and questioned His deity, and even insulted Him of His parentage. In John Chapter 8 Pharisees argued with Lord Jesus. When Jesus said that He was the light of the world, and whoever followed Him will not walk in darkness, but will have the light of life, they were about to stone Him to death; but He walked away because His time had not yet come.

Again Jesus spoke to them, saying, "I am the light of the world. Whoever follows me will not walk in darkness, but will have the light of life." So the Pharisees said to him, "You are bearing witness about yourself; your testimony is not true." (John 8:12-13 ESV)

How the Bible Came To Us

Lord Jesus explained to them that He came down from heaven, and His Father and He are one, but they rejected Him and mocked Him. He was not only mocked in His daily life but even when He was the cross. People ridiculed saying if He was the Son of God He could save Himself from the cross and save others as well. However, that was the not the purpose He came into this word for, but He came to take your sin and my sin upon Him and die on behalf of us. He suffered on behalf of us in order that we may have everlasting life.

Jesus never taught violence, yet He suffered violence at the hands of others. He never did any harm to anyone; rather He healed the sick, He helped poor and suffering, and above all He offered Himself for the sins of the whole world, and yet people rejected Him.

After much argument, and as the Pharisees still persisted in their confrontation with the Him, the Lord said "…. I told you that you would die in your sins, for unless you believe that I am he you will die in your sins". His words bear witness before the Father about the ones who rejected Him as Savior.

Today is the day of salvation. We hope to live in eternity in our glorified bodies. This salvation message and if it is rejected, then the Lord's words will resonate in heaven to judge those who did not believe Him as the Lord and Savior.

How the Bible Came To Us

BIBLIOGRAPHY

Archer Jr, Gleason L. *A Survey of Old Testament Introduction.* Chicago: Moody Press. 1984.

Bruce, F.F. *The New Testament Documents: Are They Reliable.* Grand Rapids, Michigan: W.B. Eerdmans Publishing Co. Revised 1960.

Cairns, Earle E. *Christianity Though The Centuries: A History of The Christian Church.* Grand Rapids, Michigan: Zondervan. Revised 1981.

Eerdman's Handbook To The History of Christianity. Dowley, Tim. Organizing Editor. Grand Rapids, Michigan: W. B. Eerdmans Publishing Co. 1977.

Geisler, Norman L., Nix, William E. *A General Introduction To The Bible.* Chicago: Moody Press. 1978.

Greenlee, Harold J. *Introduction To New Testament Textual Criticism.* Grand Rapids, Michigan: W.B. Eerdmans Publishing Co. 1964.

Gromacki, Robert G. *New Testament Survey.* Grand Rapids, Michigan: Baker Book House. 1974.

Harris, Laird R. *Inspiration And Canonicity Of The Bible.* Grand Rapids, Michigan: Zondervan. Revised 1969.

Harrison, Everett F. *Introduction to The New Testament.* Grand Rapids, Michigan: W.B. Eerdmans Publishing Co. Revised 1974.

House, Wayne H. *Chronological and Background Charts Of The*

How the Bible Came To Us

New Testament.
Grand Rapids, Michigan: Zondervan. 1981.

Jenson, Irving L. *Jenson's Survey Of The Old Testament.* Chicago: Moody Press. 1978.

Kenyon, Sir Frederic. *Our Bible And The Ancient Manuscripts.* London: Eyre & Spottiswoode. 1941.

Lightfoot, Neil R. *How We Got The Bible.* Grand Rapids, Michigan: Baker Book House. Third Printing 2004

McDowell, Josh. *Evidence That Demands A Verdict.* San Bernardino, California: Campus Crusade for Christ International. 1972.

Morris, Henry M. *Many Infallible Proofs.* San Diego, California: Creation-Life Publishers. 1974.

Pinnock, Clark H. *Set Forth Your Case: An Examination Of Christianity's Credentials.* Chicago: Moody Press. 1971

Schultz, Samuel J. *The Old Testament Speaks* New York, N.Y.: Harper and Row.
1970.

Tenney, Merrill C. *New Testament Survey* Grand Rapids, Michigan: W.B. Eerdmans Publishing Co. Revised 1961.

Thompson, J. A. *The Bible And Archaeology.* Grand Rapids, Michigan: W.B. Eerdmans Publishing Co. 1962.

Ungers Bible Dictionary, Chicago: Moody Press. Revised 1966.

Walton, John H. *Chronological Background Charts Of The Old Testament.* Grand Rapids, Michigan: Zondervan. 1978.

How the Bible Came To Us

Wycliffe Bible Encyclopedia, Editors: Pfeiffer, Charles F; Vos, Howard F; Rea, John; Two Volumes. Chicago: Moody Press. 1975.

Zondervan Pictorial Encyclopedia Of The Bible, General Editor: Tenney, Merrill C. Five Volumes. Grand Rapids, Michigan: Zondervan. 1976.

"dictionary." *Dictionary.com Unabridged.* Random House, Inc. 11 Jun. 2015.

---

[i] William L. Petersen, *What Text can New Yestament Textual Criticism Ultimately Reach,* in: B. Aland & J. Delobel (eds.) *New Testament Textual Criticism, Exegesis and Church History* (Pharos: Kampen, 1994), p. 137.

www.ingramcontent.com/pod-product-compliance
Lightning Source LLC
Chambersburg PA
CBHW031348040426
42444CB00005B/225